CONSPIRATORS

CONSPIRATORS

A Photographic History of Ireland's Revolutionary Underground

Shane Kenna

Published in association with

The National Library
of Ireland

and

FOUNDED IN 1828

GLASNEVIN TRUST

DARDISTOWN   GLASNEVIN   GOLDENBRIDGE
NEWLANDS CROSS   PALMERSTOWN

The Glasnevin Trust

MERCIER PRESS
IRISH PUBLISHER – IRISH STORY

MERCIER PRESS
Cork
www.mercierpress.ie

© Text: Shane Kenna, 2015

© Images: see individual images for copyright holders.

ISBN: 978 1 78117 354 1

10 9 8 7 6 5 4 3 2 1

A CIP record for this title is available from the British Library

Printed and bound in Spain.

CONTENTS

ACKNOWLEDGEMENTS   6

INTRODUCTION   7

1   FROM CONSPIRACY TO REVOLUTION   13

2   REORGANISATION AND A CONSPIRACY OF SHADOWS   69

SELECT BIBLIOGRAPHY   155

INDEX   157

ACKNOWLEDGEMENTS

This book is the culmination of a major photographic history project between myself, the National Library of Ireland, Glasnevin Cemetery and Mercier Press. I am indebted to the help, guidance and support of Katherine McSherry, George McCullough and Mary Feehan. I am exceedingly grateful to Mercier Press for giving me the opportunity to write this book and have thoroughly enjoyed the experience of working with the publishers. I would also like to thank the staff in the National Library of Ireland. I have found their assistance to be exemplary and first class. Special thanks is reserved for the team in the National Library digitisation studio. They undertook sterling work within this digitisation project and I feel the book is the better for the quality of their photographs. I would also like to thank the following people: Elizabeth M. Kirwan, Keith Murphy and Aideen Ireland.

I would like to acknowledge special thanks to Aidan Lambert for the kind support he has given me in this project and for allowing me permission to access his vast collection of Fenian materials and ephemera. I cannot thank Aidan enough for his support and advice throughout this project; it is greatly appreciated. I would like to thank all my friends and family for their unwavering support, including my mother Olive and my partner Edel Quinn, whom I thank for their continuing love, support and patience. I would also like to thank John Kenna and Liz Gillis, who gave me the idea for this project in Kilmainham Gaol, Éamon Murphy and Barry Kennerk. Barry Kennerk is an outstanding historian – his knowledge and support is greatly appreciated and I consider him one of my finest friends.

INTRODUCTION

The Irish Republican Brotherhood (IRB), also known as the Fenians, was one of the most important revolutionary organisations within Irish history and had a profound influence on the emergence of Ireland as we understand it today. Through sixty years of secretive conspiracy it bestrode Irish history like a colossus. It was a key factor in the emergence of cultural and political organisations in the late nineteenth and early twentieth centuries, played an active role in the Irish revolution of 1916–21 and was a crucial group in terms of the negotiation of the Anglo-Irish Treaty of 1921 and the emergence of the Irish Free State.

The IRB emerged from the socio-political environment of the 1840s, a decade that saw the rise of both Daniel O'Connell's Repeal Association and the Young Ireland Society. Both sought the repeal of the Act of Union, which had established the United Kingdom of Great Britain and Ireland on 1 January 1801. However, nationalist hopes for change were undermined by determined parliamentary opposition to repeal and the declining power of O'Connell, who was unwilling to consider the use of violence in his challenge to British government in Ireland. As O'Connell's influence began to wane, Ireland also faced a catastrophe in the form of the Great Famine (1845–50). Against this background, the Young Irelanders, who had been driven from the Repeal Association in July 1847, decided the time had come for radical change.

The Young Irelanders were articulate and educated; they argued for a common Irish nationality, irrespective of religious or cultural differences, an aspect of Republican ideology still traceable today. Having broken from O'Connell, they formed the Irish Confederation, but this was undermined by internal divisions over the use of violence. When radical men such as John Mitchel departed from the organisation, it was left in the hands of more moderate leaders. However, forced into action by the inaction of the government during the famine, and inspired by radical movements abroad, the Young Irelanders rebelled on 29 July 1848. This rebellion did not have popular support and in the end was nothing more than a skirmish as rebels besieged a number of policemen trapped in a widow's cottage at Ballingarry, Tipperary, but failed to capture them.

After the failure of the 1848 rebellion, the Young Ireland movement was effectively finished, with many of its leaders jailed or on the run. With the country exhausted and demoralised by the famine, the mantle of nationalist Ireland now passed to Dublin radicals led by former Young Irelander James Fintan Lalor. In 1849 he staged a revolt and planned to kidnap Queen Victoria on her visit to Dublin. However, despite his best intentions, this rebellion also descended into a small-scale skirmish, at a police barracks in Cappoquin. Despite its failure, it is important to note that several of the rebels associated with Lalor were crucial to the later development of Fenianism, including Thomas Clarke Luby and Peter Langan.

When Lalor died in December 1849 nationalist Ireland lacked a leader and revolutionary organisation disappeared. Despite this, the spirit of national independence still manifested itself through the Irish Tenants League, founded by another former Young Irelander, Charles Gavan Duffy. While advocating improved rights for tenant farmers, this League also wanted repeal of the Union. Gavan Duffy established an Irish Party which he hoped would act to further Irish national interests in parliament. Performing well in the 1852 general election, the party soon imploded when many of its members, who had campaigned on a promise of never taking a government position, promptly advanced their own careers once elected. Duffy lost faith in the project and moved to Australia, leaving a deep mistrust of constitutional nationalism in his wake.

The famine and the failure of the Young Ireland rebellion led to a massive increase in Irish emigration to America. This effectively established a nation in exile. In 1850 it was estimated that 133,000 people living in New York city were Irish born. Arriving in America, Irish emigrants were met with hostility and prejudice. This forced the Irish population there together and the nationalist movement thrived. A Directory of the Friends of Ireland society was set up prior to the 1848 rebellion and continued to exist after its collapse. Similarly Irish America established a military organisation referred to as the Irish Republican Union, which would eventually morph into the famous 9th Regiment of the New York State Militia.

While America was becoming a key component of the Irish struggle for independence, Europe was equally important to the evolution of the Fenian movement. In the mid-nineteenth century Paris was a hotbed of revolutionary activity. While many Young Irelanders escaped to America, others made for Europe and settled in Paris, including John O'Mahony, Michael Doheny and James Stephens. Doheny went to New York in 1849, but Stephens and O'Mahony stayed and associated with the revolutionary underground, studying their organisation and methodology. In 1854 O'Mahony went to New York, where he helped to found the Emmet Monument Association (EMA), a society committed to an Irish rebellion, led by John Mitchel and including his good friend Doheny. Hopeful of establishing a revolutionary movement in Ireland, the EMA dispatched Joseph Denieffe, another veteran Young Irelander, to Ireland. It was envisaged that Denieffe could make contact with existing nationalists in Ireland in conjunction with the support of the EMA, which had promised resources and support for a future rebellion. While Denieffe met with many nationalists, he became increasingly frustrated with the inactivity of the EMA and the lack of promised funds. Disheartened, he prepared to return to America, but was persuaded to continue his work by James Stephens, who had returned to Ireland in 1856. Stephens dispatched Denieffe back to America to secure a promise of definitive funding. He had been asked by the EMA to lead a revolutionary movement in Ireland and gave Denieffe a detailed list of terms for consideration, including absolute control of the new movement and payment of £100 a month for three months. Returning to Ireland Denieffe informed Stephens that the EMA accepted his terms, but could only provide £80. Agreeing to found the new movement, Stephens, Denieffe, Thomas Clarke Luby, Garret O'Shaughnessy and Peter Langan established the IRB on St Patrick's Day 1858.

The IRB was a secretive organisation initially led by a single leader, but in July 1867 a Supreme Council representative of the Irish nation and diaspora took charge of it. Its structure was cellular and divided into organisational circles to prevent infiltration by spies and informers. Each circle was led by one individual, known as an 'A' or Centre. Each 'A' had the support of nine 'B's, who in military terms represented captains. These 'B's were expected to take the place of the 'A' if he was arrested or incapacitated, meaning that the group would never be without a leader. The nine 'B's were followed by a further nine 'C's and 'D's, equivalent to sergeants and privates respectively. In theory none of the 'C's or 'D's knew the identity of the Fenian centre in their circle. Each circle was organised independently of the others, with its members supposedly not knowing each other. However, this was never really adhered to and as the IRB grew, the secrecy favoured by the organisation became harder to maintain.

All members of the IRB were expected to swear an oath to uphold the principles of the movement and strive to establish an Irish Republic:[1]

> I _____ in the presence of Almighty God, do solemnly swear allegiance to the Irish Republic, now virtually established; and that I will do my very utmost, at every risk, while life lasts, to defend its independence and integrity; and, finally, that I will yield implicit obedience in all things not contrary to the laws of God to the commands of my superior officers. So help me God. Amen.

Despite the inclusion of God in the oath, the IRB was also secularist and rejected religious differences, seeking to unite the Irish irrespective of their faith. Fenians believed that religious practice was a private affair which should not interfere with

---

1   Ryan, Desmond, *The Fenian Chief: A Biography of James Stephens* (Dublin, 1967), p. 92.

the national question. They sought the right of equal citizenship for all, based on the principle of an all-inclusive Irish nation. Differing from previous revolutionary groups, the IRB was not confined to romantics and aristocrats, but actively recruited among the working class, soldiers, shopkeepers, clerks and school teachers. Their conspiracy against British rule effectively became a movement uniting sections of the underclasses with the middle class, seeking a democratic, secular Republic. This, alongside its insistence on the use of a secret oath, brought Fenianism into conflict with the Catholic Church. Its most vocal critic was Cardinal Paul Cullen, archbishop of Dublin, who looked upon Fenianism with horror and vowed to 'wage an unrelenting war on the organisation'.[2]

The IRB continued to be aided by the Irish-American community, which was schooled in American ideas of Republicanism, particularly concepts of citizenship stressing the right to bear arms and freedom of speech and of assembly. Irish-Americans pursued a deep interest in the affairs of Ireland, firstly through the Fenian Brotherhood and later Clan na Gael. Their aim was to support the IRB with money, arms and an officer class to assist in overthrowing British rule in Ireland. A significant number of Irish-Americans resented the fact that they had been forced to emigrate, believing 'themselves to have been frozen out of their native land'.[3] This perception facilitated the development of a pervading political grievance desirous of vengeance against Britain.[4] Their nationalism was more extreme than in Ireland, and they reared their children on stories of tyranny underlined by acts of unrelenting cruelty and despotism.[5] These stories ensured the emergence of a cross-generational political grievance against Britain characterised by 'an unreasoning and yet solid feeling of inextinguishable hostility to the English system of government'.[6]

In 1867, supported by Irish-Americans through the Fenian Brotherhood, the IRB led an uprising against British rule in Ireland. Their rebellion, despite elaborate plans which included infiltration of the British Army, guerrilla warfare and frontal assault battles, effectively descended into scattered skirmishes and fizzled out. Poor military leadership undermined their plans, while the overwhelming resources of the British Army in Ireland and the pervasive presence of spies and informers working on behalf of the state to damage the IRB adversely affected the rebellion.

Despite this defeat, Fenianism did not go away and the conspirators quickly

---

2   Devoy, John, *Recollections of an Irish Rebel* (New York, 1929), p. 118.
3   Bagenal, Philip, *The American Irish and their Influence on Irish Politics* (London, 1882), p. 218.
4   Crenshaw, Martha, 'The causes of terrorism', in *Comparative Politics*, 13:4 (July 1981) p. 394.
5   Henry, George, 'An American view of Ireland,' in *Nineteenth Century: A Monthly Review,* 12:66 (August, 1882) p. 177; draft of John Devoy's recollections, undated, NLI Ms 18,014.
6   Bagenal, Philip, *The American Irish and their Influence on Irish Politics* (London, 1882), pp. 218–19.

reorganised themselves, creating a tightly knit revolutionary organisation under a Supreme Council in Ireland and the newly dominant Irish-American association Clan na Gael. In 1871 the British government actually facilitated the reorganisation of the revolutionary conspiracy. As a means of pacifying nationalist Ireland, it amnestied Fenian prisoners on the condition that they did not return to Ireland for the duration of their sentences. Many of the amnestied prisoners settled in America and joined Clan na Gael. Jeremiah O'Donovan Rossa was one of the first to be released. When he arrived in America he brought with him the greatest of all the Fenians, John Devoy. Through Devoy, Fenian activists played an instrumental role in the Land War of 1879–82, negotiated with Charles Stewart Parnell seeking a pan-nationalist front and masterminded the daring *Catalpa* escape from the impregnable Freemantle Prison in Western Australia. Devoy and O'Donovan Rossa were followed to America by a huge swathe of amnestied prisoners, many of whom remained actively committed to Irish independence. Ironically, it became evident that the British government had effectively pushed the Fenian conspiracy to a jurisdiction where it could not be controlled.

This was represented in the 1880s by increased Irish-American influence over Fenian activities in Ireland, illustrated by the dynamite campaign. Between 1881 and 1885, Fenians undertook a sustained bombing campaign in Britain against economic and symbolic targets. In addition there was a willingness amongst a minority of Fenian activists to consider political assassination as a defined tactic against British officials in Ireland. This resulted in the infamous Phoenix Park assassinations in 1882, when two of the British government's most important administrators in Ireland were assassinated in broad daylight by a group referring to themselves as The Irish National Invincibles. By the 1890s, however, the once mighty Fenian conspiracy, weakened by the Irish Parliamentary Party and Clan na Gael splits, and undermined by a policy of waiting for British difficulty to become Irish opportunity, entered into a phase of decline and soon became a shadow of its former self.

A revival of sorts took place in 1898 with the hundredth anniversary of the 1798 rebellion, followed by the outbreak of the Boer War in 1899, which offered Irish conspirators the chance to take advantage of British imperial difficulty abroad. The IRB formed an Irish brigade to fight for the Boers against Britain and its most famous member was John MacBride, later executed for his role in the Easter Rising of 1916.

With continuing financial support from Clan na Gael, as the twentieth century opened a small cabal of revolutionaries living in Belfast city decided to begin a process of reorganisation. Three of these Fenian activists – Denis McCullough, Bulmer Hobson and later Seán MacDiarmada – replaced the older figures within the movement with a younger and fresher leadership. By 1907 they were joined by Thomas James Clarke, who, after fifteen gruelling years in prison for his part in the bombing campaign in Britain, was active in the Fenian movement in America. Returning to Ireland in the early twentieth century, Clarke commanded great respect from the younger conspirators and forged a strong alliance with McCullough, Hobson and MacDiarmada. With MacDiarmada, Clarke was responsible for the greatest Fenian conspiracy – preparation for the Easter Rising of 1916. Fenianism had passed the torch of Republican idealism to a new generation, but that generation could not have made the gains it achieved between 1916 and 1921 without the sixty years of extraordinary conspiracy, resilience, idealism and self-sacrifice which their predecessors maintained.

This is the first time the Fenian conspiracy has been outlined in illustrated-book form. With it I hope to introduce the reader to the personalities and history of Irish conspiracy in the nineteenth and early twentieth centuries. This book contains many previously unseen images that belong to various national and private collections. The images include photographs, lithographic illustrations and cartoons, which introduce the conspirators and their activities and show how their opponents depicted them. It also examines the nature of the British response to the Fenian conspiracy in the nineteenth century and introduces many individuals who were previously lost to history.

The Fenian conspirators of the nineteenth century, through their activities and perseverance in trying to achieve their goals against all odds, inspired the generation which followed, who considered themselves the heirs to their Fenian forebears. This generation included Patrick Pearse, Éamonn Ceannt, Thomas MacDonagh, Michael Collins, Thomas Ashe and Joseph Mary Plunkett. It is evident that without the activities of the Fenians in the nineteenth century, the struggle for independence in the ten short years from 1913 to 1923 would not have taken place. This was graphically represented when, in 1915, Patrick Pearse delivered the graveside oration for the veteran Fenian Jeremiah O'Donovan Rossa at Glasnevin Cemetery, Dublin, famously announcing:

If there is anything that makes it fitting that I, rather than some other, rather than one of the grey-haired men who were young with him and shared in his labour and in his suffering, should speak here, it is perhaps that I may be taken as speaking on behalf of a new generation that has been re-baptised in the Fenian faith, and that has accepted the responsibility of carrying out the Fenian programme.

Shane Kenna,
Dublin, 2015

1
FROM CONSPIRACY TO REVOLUTION

Following the collapse of the disastrous 1848 rebellion and the failure of the Young Ireland Society, John O'Mahony (*left*) and James Stephens (*right*) escaped to Paris. There they associated with a revolutionary underground and a network of secret societies. O'Mahony stayed in Paris for two years before leaving for America, while James Stephens remained there until late 1855, after which he returned to Ireland. Both were instrumental in the foundation of the new Irish revolutionary conspiracy. (*Courtesy of the National Library of Ireland*)

This letter, in the handwriting of James Stephens, was written from Paris on New Year's Day, 1858, (in the early days of the movement), to Michael Doheny, and tells what could be done in the way of organizing an armed revolutionary force in Ireland if only the necessary money could be provided. The letter is incomplete, and, of course, unsigned.

Paris, January 1, 1858.

My Dear Doheny:—As this is strictly a business letter you will excuse the absence of all explanations of a personal nature. I reserve everything of the kind for some future occasion—perhaps the hour I shall grasp your hand in mine with all the truth and fervor of our hunted days.

To the point.

Presuming the information given by Mr. C. to be correct, I proceed to state the conditions on which I can accept the proposed co-operation of our transatlantic brothers, and the great personal responsibility devolving on myself. Lest you should have over-rated my capability and influence, it may be well to inform you what I am convinced I can do in a given time, always provided you are prepared to comply with my conditions, which I believe essential. Bearer of this letter leaves by to-night's mail, and I undertake to organize in three months from the date of his return here at least 10,000, of whom about 1,500 shall have firearms and the remainder pikes. These men, moreover, shall be so organized as to be available (all of them) at any one point in twenty-four hours' notice at most. It must be needless to say that such an organization as this represents the whole body of Irish Nationalists—even the indifferent would be inevitably drawn after us, the start once given. Nor do I hesitate to assert that, with the aid of the 500 brave fellows you promise, we shall have such a prospect of success as has not offered since—I cannot name the epoch of our history.

Now for the conditions. The first is money. There is a slight reproach in my words when I say: you ought to have foreseen this, knowing as you do that the men of property are not with us (of course I speak but of the national men of property), and that we are without means, you would have shown a wise foresight by sending us the nerves of organization as of war. I shall be able to borrow enough to go on with the work till I hear from you; that is, on a limited scale, and at great inconvenience to myself and friends, but anything like delay on your part will not only retard its progress, but otherwise injure the Cause and should you be unable to come into my terms, the business must be given up altogether. You must then be able to furnish from £80 to £100 a month, dating from the departure of bearer from New York. Had I a casting voice in your council, I should, moreover, suggest you sending 500 men unarmed to England, there to meet an agent who should furnish each of them with an Enfield rifle. This, of course, would involve considerable expense; but were it possible it would so stave off suspicion that we might fall on them altogether by surprise. Of course, too, this money should come from you, and I beg of you, if possible, to raise it and act on my suggestion.

A few words as to my position. I believe it essential to success that the centre of this or any similar organization should be perfectly unshackled; in other words, a provisional dictator. On this point I can conscientiously concede nothing. That I should not be worried or hampered by the wavering or imbecile it will be well to make out this in proper form, with the signature of every influential Irishman of our union.

* * * * * * *

N. B.—Bearer may be trusted unto the death.

In February 1856 O'Mahony wrote to Stephens from America proposing the establishment of a revolutionary body in Ireland. Agreeing with this initiative, Stephens set out a number of goals which he felt he could achieve and also the conditions for achieving these in the letter to Doheny, the text of which is shown here. This culminated in the foundation of the secretive IRB on 17 April 1858 and Stephens being named Chief Organiser of the Irish Republic. (*Image taken from Denieffe, Joseph*, A Personal Narrative of the Irish Revolutionary Brotherhood *(New York, 1906)*)

Thomas Clarke Luby was James Stephens' deputy in the IRB and attended its founding meeting in Dublin. The son of a Church of Ireland clergyman, he was a prominent Republican and accompanied Stephens on a recruitment tour of Ireland for the Brotherhood. (*Courtesy of the National Library of Ireland*)

When O'Mahony first arrived in America he had joined forces with other veterans of the Young Ireland Society and founded the Emmet Monument Association. The association was constituted to foment revolution in Ireland, but with little success, and it was subsumed into the Fenian Brotherhood in 1859 as an auxiliary organisation financially sponsoring the IRB. O'Mahony chose the Brotherhood's name in deference to the Fianna, legendary Irish warriors. Its headquarters were at the Moffat Mansion (*shown here*), near Times Square, New York city. (*Author's collection*)

Born in Sligo in 1827, Michael Corcoran had served with both the British Army and the Irish constabulary. In 1849 he emigrated to America and within ten years became a founder member of the Fenian Brotherhood and a member of the American Army. In 1860 he refused to allow the 69th Division of the American Army, formed in 1851 by New York Irishmen, to parade during the visit of the Prince of Wales to New York city, citing the experience of the famine and British rule in Ireland. For this he was due to be court-martialled, but with the onset of the Civil War the case was dropped. (*Courtesy of the Library of Congress, LC-DIG-cwpb-06475*)

Between 1861 and 1865 the United States was embroiled in a civil war and thousands of Irishmen joined the Union and Confederate armies. This war weakened the efficacy of the Fenian Brotherhood and significantly reduced the amount of money and support available. The 69th Division were part of the Union Army and became known as 'the Fighting Irish'. The division was mainly based in Fort Corcoran, Virginia. Above are members of the division who were captured at the Battle of Bull Run. Overleaf are officers of the 69th with Fort Corcoran behind them. (*Courtesy of the Library of Congress, LC–DIG–ppmsca-35329 and LC–DIG–ppmsca-34210*)

THE IRISH PEOPLE.

Vol. 1. No. 1.]   DUBLIN, SATURDAY, NOVEMBER 28, 1863.   PRICE {STAMPED, TWOPENCE.
{UNSTAMPED, THREE-PENCE.

Left:

In 1863 the IRB established a newspaper called *The Irish People*. The publication of a newspaper by a secret society was a dangerous move, but was rooted in the practical difficulties of the Fenian Brotherhood in relation to fund-raising during the US Civil War and the IRB's need for a reliable income. There was also the hope that the income from this newspaper would lessen the hold of the Fenian Brotherhood on the IRB, which would allow the latter organisation more independence in its actions. The photograph shows the front page of the first edition. The newspaper's editorial staff included Jeremiah O'Donovan Rossa, John O'Leary, Charles J. Kickham and Thomas Clarke Luby. (*Author's collection*)

Overleaf:

Following the establishment of *The Irish People*, Stephens travelled to America on a fund-raising tour. Before he left he gave Thomas Clarke Luby a document containing the names of a Fenian executive who would take control of the IRB in his absence. According to the historian Desmond Ryan, the document read:

> I hereby appoint Thomas Clarke Luby, John O'Leary and Charles J. Kickham, a Committee of Organization or Executive, with the same supreme control over the Home Organization (Ireland, England, Scotland, etc.) I have exercised myself. I further empower them to appoint a Committee of Military Inspection, and a Committee of Appeal and Judgment, the functions of which Committee will be made known to each member of them by the Executive. Trusting to the patriotism and ability of the Executive, I fully endorse their action beforehand, and call on every man in our ranks to support and be guided by them in all that concerns our military brotherhood. 9 March 1864, Dublin, J. STEPHENS[1]

The image shows this Fenian executive, along with several leading Fenians including O'Donovan Rossa, John O'Connor, William Francis Roantree and Denis Dowling Mulcahy. All members of *The Irish People* staff, these men represented the most senior figures within the movement in Ireland. (*Author's collection*)

---

1   Ryan, Desmond, *The Fenian Chief: A Biography of James Stephens* (Dublin, 1967), p. 195.

THE IRISH FENIAN EXECUTIVE.

Entered according to act of Congress, in the year 1866, by WILLIAM C. BLELOCH, in the Clerk's Office of the District Court of the United States for the Eastern District of Pennsylvania.

Born in Rosscarbery, West Cork, Jeremiah O'Donovan Rossa was a founder member of the Phoenix National and Literary Society, established in 1856 as a forum for discussing and debating Republican ideas. He was one of the IRB's first recruits and actively worked on recruiting men into the organisation and establishing an oath-bound network in West Cork. Arrested in December 1858, he was imprisoned without trial until July 1859. He was appointed business manager of *The Irish People* newspaper upon its inception, which meant that he was responsible for its circulation, dispatching the newspaper at home and abroad, paying the staff and ensuring that the paper arrived at newsagents promptly. Later he wrote articles under the pseudonym 'Anthony the Jobbler' and produced poetry, such as his famous 'The Soldier of Fortune'. One of his leading articles for the newspaper, 'The Martyr Nation', stated:

The fact that the Irish people are being today destroyed – some of them in soul and body stares us in the face … instead of flying, we believe it to be our duty to remain in the old land, face the evil, and meet the destroyer with his own weapons … we do not contemplate Ireland Catholic or Protestant – we contemplate her free and independent; and we extend the love and fellowship, to every man, of every class and creed, who would endeavour to make it so.

(*Courtesy of the National Library of Ireland*)

Above:

On 14 September 1865 the police raided the offices of *The Irish People*, seizing the printing press and important documentation. Following this raid widespread arrests were made. An informer, Pierce Nagle, who discovered a letter claiming rebellion was imminent, had prompted the authorities into action. The image shows an artist's impression of the raid on the newspaper. (*Courtesy of Aidan Lambert*)

Right and overleaf:

The images on the following four pages show Fenian prisoners photographed in Mountjoy Prison in 1865–66. Some of these were arrested as a result of the raid on *The Irish People*, others as a result of the suspension of the Habeas Corpus Act. (*Courtesy of the New York Public Libraries*)

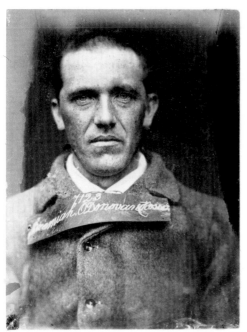

Jerh. O'Donovan Rossa.

Bryan Dillon.

Thomas Duggan.

Chas. Underwood O'Connell.

27

John Sheehan

James Sweeny

James Neill.

James O'Neille

Bernard O'Kane.

William Ryan.

Henry Broughton

James Mooney.

Edward Finn.

Myles Taylor.

James McConvill,
American Service.

Thomas Maher.

Denis Dowling Mulcahy, the sub-editor, was also arrested as part of the police raid on *The Irish People*. Sentenced to ten years imprisonment, he was released from custody in January 1871. (*Courtesy of the National Library of Ireland*)

Patrick Haybourne was born in Dublin in 1841 and was a barber in the Liberties. His family was steeped in radical traditions and his father was an enthusiastic supporter of Young Ireland in the 1840s. A prominent member of the IRB, Haybourne used his barber shop on Dublin's Thomas Street to store arms. He was arrested in December 1865 during a raid on his premises. Eventually settling in New York city, Haybourne continued as a barber and remained active within Irish-American Republicanism. (*Courtesy of the National Library of Ireland*)

George Archdeacon was a book-seller and newspaper vendor, who was arrested in Liverpool in November 1865. The IRB had a powerful network throughout England and had strong support amongst the Irish in the north of the country, in cities such as Liverpool, Manchester and Newcastle. Archdeacon sold *The Irish People* from his shop on Bidder Street in Liverpool and was the Head Centre of the IRB in that city. (*Courtesy of the National Library of Ireland*)

John Hughes was arrested in 1866 and imprisoned at Crumlin Road Gaol, Belfast. This photograph was taken in Mountjoy Prison, Dublin. (*Courtesy of the National Library of Ireland*)

Patrick Walters was twenty years of age when he was arrested under the suspension of the Habeas Corpus Act. Walters lived on Great Britain Street (now Parnell Street), Dublin, and it was noted that he had pierced ears and a cut mark on his left eyebrow. Note that he is smiling for his mugshot. This is representative of the novelty of photography for many Fenian prisoners, the camera being a relatively new invention. (*Courtesy of the National Library of Ireland*)

Morgan Burke was twenty-nine years of age in this photograph and, like Walters, is smiling for his mugshot. Originally from Dunmanway in County Cork, he had recently arrived back in Ireland from America when he was arrested on 12 March 1867. Burke was released in 1868 on condition that he return to the United States. (*Courtesy of the National Library of Ireland*)

James Stephens was arrested on 11 November 1865 in Sandymount, County Dublin, where he had been staying under the alias of Mr Herbert. The photograph is a prison shot of Stephens. Defending himself in court he boldly announced, 'I defy and despise any punishment which could be inflicted on me!'[1] (*Courtesy of the National Library of Ireland*)

---

1 Ryan, Mark F., *Fenian Memories* (Dublin, 1945), p. 66.

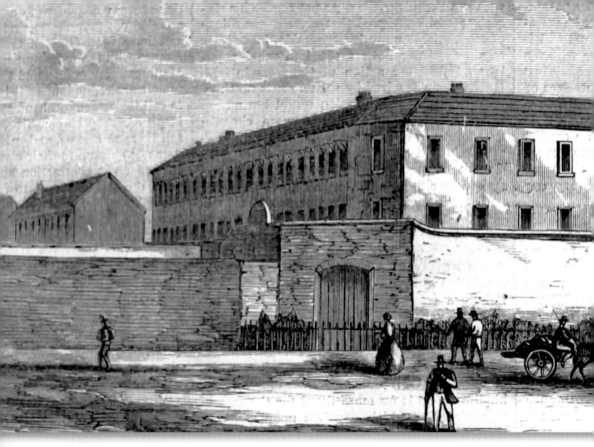

Above:

Stephens escaped from Richmond Bridewell (*shown above*) on 24 November. Two prison guards who belonged to the IRB, Daniel Byrne and John Breslin, facilitated his escape. The two guards had been supplied with copied keys by Dublin Fenian Michael Lambert, an instrument maker and jeweller. Overnight Stephens' escape became a sensational news story and bill heads were posted in Dublin seeking his arrest. Despite a significant police operation and the utilisation of informers, Stephens could not be found. The Fenian chief had made his way to Britain and then on to France, from where he escaped to America. (*Courtesy of Aidan Lambert*)

Opposite:

On 15 May 1866 Stephens received an impressive reception at Jones' Wood, Manhattan, New York city. Thousands of Irish-Americans assembled to show their support for the Chief Organiser of the Irish Republic and paid an admittance of 50 cent. They were enthralled by Stephens' recollections of his escape, with *The New York Times* stating that 'he had braved the dangers of an escape from Ireland through Saxon bayonets.'[1] (*Courtesy of Aidan Lambert*)

---

1 *The New York Times*, 16 May 1866.

HARPER'S WEEKLY.

A JOURNAL OF CIVILIZATION.

Vol. IX.—No. 462.]   NEW YORK, SATURDAY, NOVEMBER 4, 1865.   [SINGLE COPIES TEN CENTS.
$4.00 PER YEAR IN ADVANCE.

Entered according to Act of Congress, in the Year 1865, by Harper & Brothers, in the Clerk's Office of the District Court for the Southern District of New York.

MEETING OF THE FENIAN CONGRESS IN THE ASSEMBLY BUILDING, PHILADELPHIA.—[See Page 694.]

Opposite:

In October 1865 the Fenian Brotherhood had held its first post-Civil War convention, in Philadelphia. This image shows an artist's representation of the convention. The meeting had been noticeable for the great animosity between two emergent factions in the Brotherhood, one led by John O'Mahony, the other by William Roberts. O'Mahony favoured an Ireland-first policy, with the Brotherhood directing its actions towards Ireland. By contrast, Roberts believed that the Brotherhood should use its power against Canada. Seeing this growing division in America, Stephens insisted that an Irish rebellion was necessary in 1865. This temporarily prevented a split within the Brotherhood, but placed tremendous pressure on the organisation at home, particularly after the suppression of *The Irish People* and the widespread arrests.

Adopting a new constitution, the Brotherhood established a parliament of sorts, including a Senate and House of Representatives. The convention voted to abolish the position formerly occupied by O'Mahony as Head Centre of the Brotherhood and replaced it with an elected president. This position was won by O'Mahony, although his powers were restricted by Roberts' faction. (*Author's collection*)

Stephens' arrival in America failed to heal the growing split in the Fenian Brotherhood. Following the suppression of *The Irish People*, William Roberts (*right*) believed that Irish-American involvement in Ireland was foolhardy and endorsed an invasion of Canada, hoping to provoke a war between Britain and the USA and thereby make a successful insurrection in Ireland more possible. (*Courtesy of the National Library of Ireland*)

General Thomas Sweeney planned to lead a Fenian raid into Canada in 1866, but failed to do so. Born in County Cork, he had seen service in the American-Mexican war and had been wounded in the American Civil War, distinguishing himself at the Battle of Shiloh in 1862. Nicknamed 'fighting Tom', Sweeney had lost his right arm at the Battle of Churubusco, Indiana. (*Courtesy of the National Library of Ireland*)

On 2 June 1866 a Fenian army under the command of Colonel John O'Neill invaded Canada and was confronted by Canadian troops at Ridgeway, Ontario. In what became known as the Battle of Ridgeway, the Fenian army routed the Canadians and seized Ridgeway, but several hours later withdrew to Fort Erie. After a significant skirmish with Canadian militia, the Fenians took Fort Erie, but then O'Neill retreated back to New York State due to an expected assault by the British Army and Canadian militia. The main image shows a dramatic reconstruction of the Battle of Ridgeway, while the inset depicts a caricature of the same event, heralding the '*masterly* retreat of the Queen's Own'. (*Courtesy of the Library of Congress, LC-DIG-pga-03244 and LC-USZ62-89623*)

The Fenian invasion of Canada resulted in 134 casualties. In total 31 died and 103 were injured as a result of the fighting. In this photograph Canadian militia can be seen standing over the body of a dead Fenian. (*Courtesy of the Canadian Archive*)

John Devoy, who had played a role in the planning of Stephens' escape from imprisonment, had joined the IRB at eighteen. With his boyhood friend J. J. O'Kelly, he enlisted in the French Foreign Legion and served in Algeria. Returning to Ireland in 1862, Devoy headed an incredible conspiracy where Fenianism infiltrated the British Army. Known as Chief Organiser of the British Army, a title which Devoy disliked, he recruited thousands of Fenians within the British Army in Ireland into the IRB. His idea was that these soldier Fenians would defect at the time of a future rebellion, bringing with them their valuable military skills and weapons. In 1866 he planned to use soldier Fenians in the 61st (South Gloucestershire) Regiment to seize Dublin in a coup and hold out for Fenian reinforcements. However, for some unexplained reason, the plan was abandoned. (*Courtesy of the National Library of Ireland*)

In February 1866 Devoy was arrested in Pilsworth's Pub, James Street, Dublin. He was with a company of soldier Fenians. His arrest had been accomplished through the machinations of an informer, Patrick Foley. This photograph was taken in Mountjoy Prison, Dublin, following his arrest. (*Courtesy of the National Library of Ireland*)

The British government was horrified to learn that Fenianism had infiltrated the British Army. As a result court martials were used against suspected soldier Fenians and affected regiments were sent out of the country. A court martial was held at the Royal Barracks, Dublin (*shown above*), led by Colonel Brett of the British Army, and twelve British Army soldiers were found guilty of mutiny and involvement in Fenian conspiracy. They received sentences including life imprisonment and deportation. (*Courtesy of Aidan Lambert*)

Between 15 and 17 December 1866 there were several Fenian meetings in New York city, where the power of Stephens within the movement was effectively stripped and handed to Colonel Thomas Kelly (*pictured*). Travelling to England, Kelly established a headquarters in London and facilitated the establishment of a Provisional Government for Ireland. On 10 February 1867 a Republican proclamation (*opposite*) was issued denouncing monarchical government, condemning religious sectarianism, appealing to the British working class for support and declaring the Irish Republic. (*Courtesy of Aidan Lambert*)

We have suffered centuries of outrage, enforced poverty, and bitter misery. Our rights and liberties have been trampled on by an alien aristocracy, who, treating us as foes, usurped our lands, and drew away from our unfortunate country all material riches. The real owners of the soil were removed to make room for cattle, and driven across the ocean to seek the means of living, and the political rights denied to them at home, while our men of thought and action were condemned to loss of life and liberty. But we never lost the memory and hope of a national existence. We appealed in vain to the reason and sense of justice of the dominant powers.

Our mildest remonstrances were met with sneers and contempt. Our appeals to arms were always unsuccessful.

Today, having no honourable alternative left, we again appeal to force as our last resource. We accept the conditions of appeal, manfully deeming it better to die in the struggle for freedom than to continue an existence of utter serfdom.

All men are born with equal rights, and in associating to protect one another and share public burdens, justice demands that such associations should rest upon a basis which maintains equality instead of destroying it.

We therefore declare that, unable longer to endure the curse of Monarchical Government, we aim at founding a Republic based on universal suffrage, which shall secure to all the intrinsic value of their labour.

The soil of Ireland, at present in the possession of an oligarchy, belongs to us, the Irish people, and to us it must be restored.

We declare, also, in favour of absolute liberty of conscience, and complete separation of Church and State.

We appeal to the Highest Tribunal for evidence of the justness of our cause. History bears testimony to the integrity of our sufferings, and we declare, in the face of our brethren, that we intend no war against the people of England – our war is against the aristocratic locusts, whether English or Irish, who have eaten the verdure of our fields – against the aristocratic leeches who drain alike our fields and theirs.

Republicans of the entire world, our cause is your cause. Our enemy is your enemy. Let your hearts be with us. As for you, workmen of England, it is not only your hearts we wish, but your arms.

Remember the starvation and degradation brought to your firesides by the oppression of labour. Remember the past, look well to the future, and avenge yourselves by giving liberty to your children in the coming struggle for human liberty.

Herewith we proclaim the Irish Republic.

The Provisional Government

While Kelly was acting chief executive of the Irish Republic, the Frenchman Gustave Paul Cluseret (*pictured*) led his military command. Cluseret had achieved the rank of brigadier general in the Union Army and had made an agreement with Stephens that he would take control of a Fenian army if 10,000 men could be relied upon to take action in Ireland. Kelly wanted to keep Cluseret within his military staff and agreed to maintain the brigadier general's terms with Stephens. (*Courtesy of the Library of Congress, LC-DIG-cwpb-04620*)

Described by John Devoy as 'an eccentric, self-willed man, with the guerrilla habit of doing what he thought proper and often disobeying orders', Captain John McCafferty (*pictured*) planned to lead a raid on Chester Castle in England on 11 February 1867. The IRB intended to seize 300 rifles and 30,000 rounds of ammunition, cannon, shells and balls, but the raid did not take place because an informer, John Joseph Corydon, undermined the plot. (*Courtesy of the National Library of Ireland*)

In 1866 John Flood, a journalist and barrister, actively smuggled rifles from America to Ireland. Following the failure of the Chester Castle raid, Flood sailed to Ireland with McCafferty, but both were arrested at Dublin port on 23 February 1867. Transported to Australia on 12 October, Flood was imprisoned in Freemantle. On his release he settled permanently in Western Australia and became a share broker, insurer and newspaper editor. Becoming a man of means, he also bred horses and was nominated for election to the Queensland parliament twice, but was unsuccessful on both occasions. He remained active within the IRB in Australia. (*Courtesy of the National Library of Ireland*)

Another of the Fenians involved in the plans for the Chester Castle raid was Michael Davitt. Born on 25 March 1846 in Straide, County Mayo, Davitt became one of the most famous Fenians of the nineteenth century. Following the eviction of his parents from their small farm in 1850, his family moved to England, where they settled at Haslingden in Lancashire. At age eleven Davitt was working in a cotton mill and lost his right arm when it was trapped in a cogwheel. In 1858 he started evening classes at the Mechanics' Institute, where he had the benefit of a library and newspapers. There he developed a love for Irish history and read about radical politics, particularly Chartism. He was sworn into the IRB in 1865 and was a senior figure within the Northern England Fenian network. Davitt was arrested on 14 May 1870 while attempting to purchase revolvers. After seven years in prison he was released on a ticket of leave and returned to Ireland in January 1878. (*Courtesy of the Davitt Museum*)

THE FENIAN VOLUNTEER.

Published in America in 1866 by Currier and Ives, this image is an interpretation of how it was hoped a future Fenian rebellion would overthrow British rule in Ireland. A Fenian Volunteer wearing the blazer of the Union Army is stomping on the British flag. Unfortunately for the Fenians it proved impossible to live up to this idealised view of a rebellion. (*Courtesy of Aidan Lambert*)

Beginning on 5 March, the 1867 Fenian rebellion was disastrous and blighted by a scarcity of leadership and weapons. Any possible chance of success had been thwarted by a series of arrests and deportations of key figures within the IRB executive and the removal of infiltrated British Army regiments abroad. A further problem for the organisers of the rebellion was the fact that the IRB, despite its insistence on secrecy, had been infiltrated by informers who gave detailed accounts of Fenian plans and preparations to the authorities. The actual rebellion, rather than being a serious threat to British rule within Ireland, was in fact a series of uncoordinated skirmishes between police and the Fenian army. The principal points of action were in Counties Louth, Cork, Tipperary, Limerick, Clare and Dublin. In Dublin the fighting was centred at Stepaside, Glencullen and Tallaght. This image shows a dramatic reinterpretation of the Battle of Tallaght, where three Fenian columns separately engaged local police under Sub-Inspector Burke. Burke, seen on the far right, had fourteen constables and a head constable under his command. (*Courtesy of Aidan Lambert*)

CONSTABULARY BARRACKS AT ROSSKEENE, BURNT BY THE FENIANS.

These images show reconstructions of confrontations in the Tipperary countryside during the rebellion. (*Courtesy of the National Library of Ireland*)

Colonel Octave Fariola, appointed by Cluseret as a military adjutant, was a soldier of fortune and had hoped to lead a guerrilla campaign during the 1867 rebellion. With the obvious failure of the rebellion he escaped to London, where he was arrested, on the word of an informer, on Oxford Street. Four months later Fariola was brought to Ireland and imprisoned at Kilmainham Gaol, Dublin. He told the authorities all he knew about the conspiracy and was released on 20 December 1867. (*Courtesy of the National Library of Ireland*)

John Edward Kelly was active in skirmishes between Fenians and the police in Cork during the rebellion. He was sentenced to hang; however, his execution was commuted to life imprisonment and he was transported to Freemantle in Western Australia. Kelly was conditionally pardoned in 1869. (*Courtesy of the National Library of Ireland*)

On 4 May 1867 James Dunne (alias Michael Cody) was arrested on Grafton Street, Dublin, with a loaded seven-chamber pistol. Police discovered a document containing the names and addresses of the judges presiding over the trials of Fenian prisoners upon his person. It was speculated that he was the leader of an assassination committee within Fenianism. Dunne was sentenced to twenty years' imprisonment and was transported to Western Australia. He was released in 1871 and remained active in the Irish conspiracy there, particularly Sydney, until he moved to Boston in 1876. (*Courtesy of the National Library of Ireland*)

Fitted out by the Fenian Brotherhood, *Erin's Hope* arrived in Ireland on 20 May 1867. Its cargo included experienced Irish-American officers, ammunition and supplies. However, with the rebellion already suppressed, it was too late for it to be of any use, and all it could do was drop off the officers. Within a day they had been arrested. (*Courtesy of Kilmainham Gaol Museum, 07GA–1A26–12*)

Captain John F. Kavanagh was the naval commander of *Erin's Hope*. After dropping off the Fenian leaders, *Erin's Hope* returned to America. (*Courtesy of Kilmainham Gaol Museum, 07GA-1A26-05*)

Opposite:
When the *Erin's Hope* passengers disembarked at Helvick, near Dungarvan, County Waterford, they were arrested within a day and interned in Kilmainham Gaol and Mountjoy Prison, Dublin. Augustine Costello, who was a naturalised American citizen, argued that as an American he could not be tried for treason felony and that, if the state persisted in the trial, he would demand a mixed jury of Irish and Americans. The court refused to grant his request on the basis that 'he who was once under the allegiance of the English Crown remains so forever'. This caused great offence within America. On 12 May 1870, as a result of pressure from America, the British government passed the Naturalisation Act and concluded a treaty with the American government asserting that citizens of each country could naturalise in either America or Britain and be entitled to the rights of citizenship irrespective of their original birth. The image shows a number of the arrested men: Augustine Costello, Michael Walsh, John Hanley, Bryan Courtney and — Nugent. (*Courtesy of the National Library of Ireland*)

Augustus F. Costelloe

Michl. Walsh

John Sharley

Nugent

Bryan Courtney

On 11 September 1867 Colonel Kelly and an associate, Timothy Deasy, were arrested in Manchester. The following week, as they were being transported in a Black Maria police van, a Fenian party attempted to secure their release. Firing into the police van through the lock to force open the door, they accidently killed a police sergeant, James Brett. Kelly and Deasy escaped, but three men who were involved in the attack on the Black Maria were captured – William Allen, Michael Larkin and Michael O'Brien. (*Courtesy of Aidan Lambert*)

Allen, Larkin and O'Brien were executed for the killing of Sergeant Brett, despite being innocent of the killing itself. They became known as the Manchester Martyrs and their execution on 23 November 1867 was the first political execution in Britain since that of Robert Emmet in 1803. (*Courtesy of the National Library of Ireland*)

A commemorative card for the Manchester Martyrs, with Larkin on the left, Allen in the middle and O'Brien on the right. (*Courtesy of the Library of Congress, LC-DIG-pga-01413*)

AN APPEAL

TO

ENGLAND

AGAINST THE EXECUTION OF THE
CONDEMNED FENIANS.

BY

ALGERNON CHARLES SWINBURNE,
AUTHOR OF POEMS AND BALLADS,
ATALANTA IN CALYDON,
Chastelard, &c.

MANCHESTER:
REPRINTED FROM THE "MORNING STAR."
1867.

Algernon Charles Swinburne was an English playwright who had supported Allen, Larkin and O'Brien and wrote a sympathetic pamphlet: *An Appeal to England against the Execution of the Condemned Fenians.* (*Courtesy of the National Library of Ireland*)

Despite the failure of 1867, the IRB was still committed to overthrowing British rule in Ireland. A veteran of the 1867 rebellion, Patrick Lennon was the head of an assassination circle within the Fenian network seeking to root out informers. He was implicated in the shooting of two policemen on 31 October 1867 at Temple Bar, Dublin, and was arrested soon after. (*Courtesy of the National Library of Ireland*)

Lennon was arrested because of Jack Cade O'Loughlin. O'Loughlin was arrested in Dublin on 1 November 1867 and was found in the possession of a loaded six-chamber colt revolver. He turned informer to Dublin Castle and claimed that Lennon had shot the policemen. For this he received a reduced prison term and resettlement abroad. (*Courtesy of the National Archives of Ireland*)

James McGrath was an ally of Lennon and had raised money for his defence. The money was used to influence witnesses to provide Lennon with believable alibis. Tried in February 1868, Lennon was acquitted due to a lack of evidence. McGrath himself was arrested on 18 March 1868, when police found Fenian documents and a loaded five-chamber revolver amongst other weapons in his house. (*Courtesy of the National Archives of Ireland*)

Posing as a representative of the Chilean government in England, Ricard O'Sullivan Burke had been organising an arms importation scheme for the IRB. Arrested along with another IRB man, Joseph Casey, on 20 November 1867, he was imprisoned in Clerkenwell House of Detention. (*Courtesy of the National Library of Ireland*)

On 13 December 1867 London IRB activists tried to rescue O'Sullivan Burke and Casey. Using gunpowder, they hoped to blow a hole in the prison wall, allowing the Fenian prisoners to escape from the adjacent yard. However, they used too much explosive and blew down sixty yards of the prison wall. Twelve people, including children, were killed and more than forty were injured. (*Courtesy of the National Library of Ireland*)

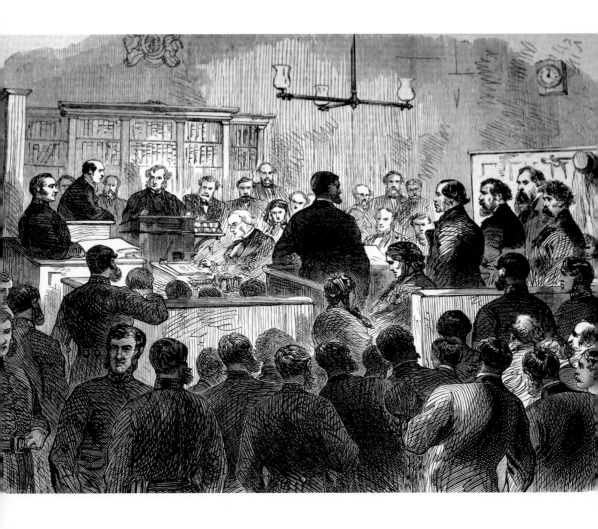

Between 20 and 27 April 1868, Michael Barrett, William Desmond, Timothy Desmond, John O'Keefe and Nicholas English were tried for involvement in the Clerkenwell bombing. A representation of the trial is shown above. At the trial, one of their comrades, Patrick Mullaney, turned informer and alleged that Michael Barrett had triggered the bomb. This was supported by a voluntary statement written by English. Barrett was found guilty and sentenced to be hanged, while William and Timothy Desmond, John O'Keefe and Nicholas English were pronounced not guilty. Michael Barrett was hanged at Newgate Gaol, London, on 26 May 1868. His execution made history as this was the last public execution in Britain. Mullaney was rewarded for his evidence with a new identity and safe transport to Australia. (*Courtesy of Aidan Lambert*)

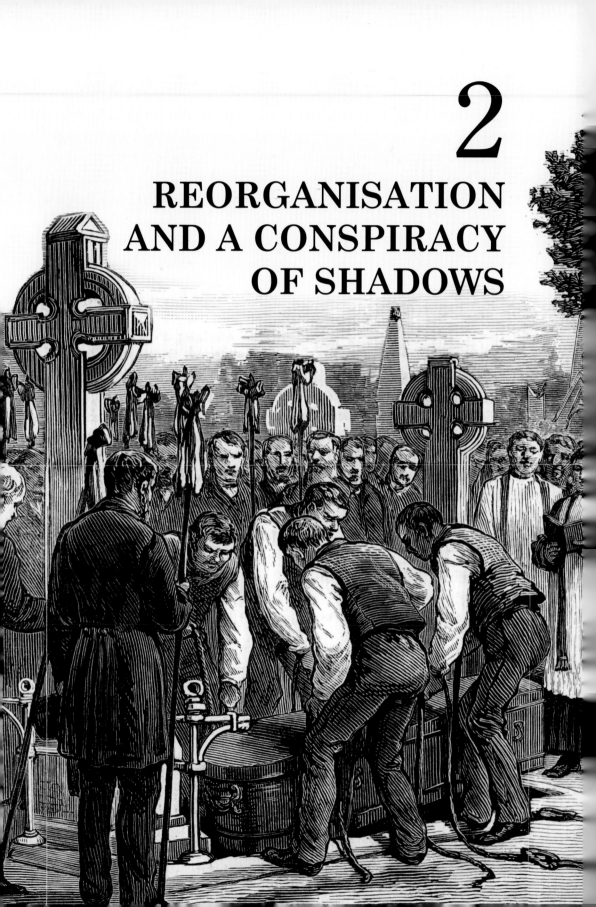

2

REORGANISATION
AND A CONSPIRACY
OF SHADOWS

Following the suppression of the 1867 rebellion the Fenians began an internal process of reorganisation to fight for self-determination. As part of this process they established a Supreme Council as a representative governing body and army council to organise the movement. It was generally agreed amongst most leading IRB figures that no one man should ever hold complete power in the organisation.

The Supreme Council's first message, in April 1868, addressed the Irish people and declared that 'the right of Ireland to self government and independent nationhood is inherent and inalienable.'[1] The council, while seeking to establish the concept of Irish sovereignty, also established in principle the concept of ignoring the organisation of British rule in Ireland. Of importance in this strategy was the fact that the council referred to itself as the Supreme Council of the Irish Republic and assigned itself the authority to legislate for, bind and claim obedience from the Irish Army or the Irish people.[2] This language suggests that in terms of ideology the Supreme Council had declared the Irish Republic, and as such saw itself as the supreme governing body of that institution, deriving its support, legitimacy and authority from the 'army and people of Ireland'.[3] The following year the council admitted in its constitution that it was the government of the Irish Republic assembled in the name of that Republic.[4]

The Supreme Council was thus ignoring reality in its ideology; in 1868 British rule in Ireland was shaken but by no means on the brink of collapse. The Irish Republic established by the council did not have legitimacy from the Irish people: few knew of its existence and it was concocted, established and led by an assemblage of revolutionaries, few of whom the people knew. This was made clear by the fact that the majority of the Irish people had no desire to fight to establish such an institution. While the IRB tacitly refused to admit this – and to do so would have been to shatter the illusion of its legitimacy – it nonetheless recognised this as an inescapable fact. In the very message that declared the Irish Republic, the IRB pointed out that the movement was committed to opposing premature action on behalf of the Republic and restrained members from committing acts of violence or outrage in its name. In this respect, any violent act carried out in the name of Irish self-determination which the council deemed inappropriate and premature was to be opposed. This attitude was reflected in 1873 when the IRB, in its process of internal reorganisation, initiated a new constitution,

---

1   Moody, T. W. and O'Broin, Leon, 'The IRB Supreme Council, 1868–78: Select Documents', in *Irish Historical Studies*, Vol. XIX (1974–75), p. 299.

2   *Ibid.*

3   *Ibid.*

4   Constitution of the IRB Supreme Council, 18 August 1869, and Fenian papers 6001R (NAI).

whereby it forbade itself from organising a rebellion against British rule on the island of Ireland, unless that rebellion had the majority support of the Irish people as to 'the fit hour of inaugurating a war against England.'[5] The IRB calculated that it would wait for the opportunity to attack British rule at a point of British difficulty on the international scene, and when supported by popular opinion.

For those Fenians jailed for their involvement in the rebellion and its aftermath, an amnesty campaign, carried out by Irish nationalists and led by the former unionist Isaac Butt through the Amnesty Association, successfully put the question of the release of Fenian prisoners onto the political agenda. Such was the appeal of the Amnesty Association that it succeeded in causing Prime Minister Gladstone and the Liberal Party embarrassment arising from the ill-treatment of Fenian internees. The government decided to establish a commission of inquiry under Lord Devon, which proved Amnesty Association claims of mistreatment of the Fenian prisoners, particularly O'Donovan Rossa. On 28 November 1870 *The Irish Times* reported that Lord Devon had finalised his report and handed it to the home secretary, leaving Britain, Ireland and Irish-America looking on with interest as it was speculated there would be an amnesty before Christmas.[6] When the amnesty arrived, however, it was controversial, as Fenian prisoners would not be given a full amnesty: their release was conditional and they were to agree to absent themselves from Ireland for the duration of their sentence.

Some of the first prisoners to be released were O'Donovan Rossa, Devoy, Henry Mulleda, John McClure and Charles Underwood O'Connell. These five chose the United States of America for their conditional exile and, on boarding the transatlantic steamer *Cuba*, they became known as the Cuba Five. Their arrival in the United States heralded a new era in Irish-American Fenianism, as they quickly joined the most important revolutionary organisation in Irish-America, Clan na Gael.

According to Devoy, Clan na Gael was formally founded by Jerome Collins, an Irish immigrant from County Cork, in the home of James Sheedy, Hester Street, New York, on 20 June 1867.[7] The date of Clan na Gael's formation was incredibly symbolic – it was the anniversary of the birth of Theobald Wolfe Tone, the father of Irish Republicanism, born in 1763. The organisation's name was chosen by Samuel Cavanagh; it was also called the United Brotherhood in English. Devoy asserted that

---

5   Moody, T. W. and O'Broin, Leon, 'The IRB Supreme Council, 1868–78: Select Documents', in *Irish Historical Studies*, Vol. XIX (1974–75), p. 314.

6   *The Irish Times*, 28 November 1870.

7   Devoy, John, 'The Story of the Clan na Gael', *Gaelic American* (29 November 1924), p. 4.

all Fenian organisations on both sides of the Atlantic were represented at the inaugural meeting.

While Clan na Gael was ostensibly established to facilitate the creation of the Irish Republic, it also had a more immediate ambition as it sought to unite fractured Irish-American Fenianism into one significant bloc. To do this Collins developed a plan to abduct Prince Arthur of Connaught and hold him hostage for the release of nationalist prisoners in British gaols, using people from both factions of the Fenian Brotherhood and the IRB. The plan was not successful, but in its immediate aftermath it was decided to 'effect an organisation that would afford a common meeting ground for members of both factions of the Fenian Brotherhood at which they would keep the peace'.[8] As a result the Clan formed the Napper Tandy Club in New York. By the 1870s more branches followed, each numbered in the order of their organisation; by 1876 the movement claimed a conservative estimate of over 11,000 members. Each club was to be referred to as a camp and was to be named after a famous Irishman, such as 'the Robert Emmet, or the Wolfe Tone or the Thomas Davis club.'[9] Unlike previous Irish-American incarnations of Fenianism, Clan na Gael remained entirely secretive and was not a public fraternal organisation.

Examining the evolution of Clan na Gael, the British government correctly believed that it was 'the corresponding organisation to the IRB in the United States ... the members of which all pledge themselves by the most solemn oath to take up arms to establish an Irish Republic'. This was a correct assessment; the Clan's constitution noted that its object was the 'attainment of complete and absolute independence of Ireland, by the overthrow of English domination; a total separation from that country and the complete severance of all political connection with it.'[10]

---

8   *Ibid.*

9   *Ibid.*

10 Le Caron, Henri, *Twenty-five Years in the Secret Service: the Recollections of a Spy* (London, 1892), p. 110.

AMENDED
CONSTITUTION OF THE IRISH REPUBLICAN BROTHERHOOD.

Whereas The Irish People have never ceased to struggle for the recovery of their independence since the date of its destruction and **whereas** it has on this 17th Day of March, the day of our Patron Saint, St. Patrick, 1873 been resolved by a convention of Irish Patriots,held in Dublin and representing associations of Irishmen existing in various parts of Ireland, England and Scotland to amend the Constitution of the present Irish Revolutionary Organisation for the purpose of overthrowing English power in Ireland, and of establishing an independent Irish Republic. Said organisation being known as The Irish Republican Brotherhood and governed by a Council by a council entitled "The Supreme Council of the Irish Republican Brotherhood and Government of the Irish Republic". The following is declared to be and promulgated as the Amended Constitution of the Irish Republican Brotherhood and of the Supreme Council of the Irish Republican Brotherhood and Government of the Irish Republic.

CONSTITUTION OF THE IRISH REPUBLICAN BROTHERHOOD.
----

1   The I.R.B. is and shall be composed of Irishmen, irrespective of class or creed resident in Ireland,England,Scotland,America Australia and in all other lands where Irishmen live,who are willing to labour for the establishment of a free and Independent Republican Government in Ireland.

2   The I.R.B. whilst labouring to prepare Ireland for the task of recovering her independence by force of arms shall confine itself in time of peace to the exercise of moral influences, - the cultivation of union and brotherly love amongst Irishmen - the propagation of Republican Principles and the spreading of a knowledge

The Supreme Council of the IRB included representatives of the Irish provinces, Scotland and Northern England. Above and overleaf is the new constitution which it adopted as its governing rules. (*Courtesy of the National Library of Ireland*)

of the national rights of Ireland.

3 The I.R.B. shall await the decision of the Irish Nation as expressed by a majority of the Irish people as to the fit hour of mangurating a war against England and shall pending such an emergency, le^d its support to every movement calculated to advance the cause of Irish independence, consistently with the preservation of its own integrity.

4 The mode of initiating members into the I.R.B. shall be the rendering of the following Oath of Allegiance to its Government:-

> "In the presence of God. I................do
> solemnly swear that I will do my utmost to
> establish the national independence of Ireland,
> and that I will bear true allegiance to the
> Supreme Council of the Irish Republican Brotherhood
> and Government of the Irish Republic and implicitly
> obey the Constitution of the Irish Republican
> Brotherhood and all my superior officers and that
> I will preserve inviolable the secrets of the
> organisation".

5 No one shall be inducted into the I.R.B. whose character for sobriety, truth, valour and obedience to Authority cannot bear scrutiny.

6 Each member of the I.R.B. shall contribute according to his means for the production of war materials and also towards the expense of keeping up communication in the different divisions of the I.R.B. and for maintaining the efficiency of the Supreme Council.

7 In every case where arms are lost through negligence the department through the neglect of which the loss has occurred shall be responsible for the value of the arms.

8 The members of the I.R.B. resident in towns or parishes shall be directed and governed by an officer to be entitled a centre and to be elected by the members of the I.R.B. each body of members electing

the centre for their own town or parish.

9   The members and centres of the I.R.B. shall be directed and governed by an officer to be entitled a County Centre and to be elected by the Centres of the respective counties, and in England and Scotland the towns shall be grouped into districts corresponding in population to the counties in Ireland and each district shall be directed and governed by a District Centre who shall be elected by the Centres of his district.

10   The I.R.B. shall be divided into seven electoral divisions - to wit - Leinster, Ulster, Munster, Connaught, North of England, South of England and Scotland and in each division one Civil and one Military Secretary shall be elected by the County or district Centres and the duty of the Civil Secretary shall be to act in all respects as deputy of the member of the Supreme Council of his division and in the event of the removal of said member by the act of the enemy, disability or death the Civil Secretary shall exercise authority in the division untill a new member of the Supreme Council shall have been elected in the manner provided for in the Constitution of the Supreme Council; and the duties of the Military Secretary shall be to execute all orders received by him in relation to the procuring, distribution and safe keeping of arms and ammunition.

11.   The term of office of all members of the I.R.B. shall be subject to removal at any time by a two thirds vote of the electoral body.

12.   The divisional officers shall have power to make all bye-laws framed in accordance with the spirit of the Constitution - which they may deem necessary for the purpose of local organisation.

13.   Each County or District Centre shall on or before the last day in each month send in a report of the position and progress of affairs to the Civil Secretary of his division who shall forthwith send it to the member of the Supreme Council for the Division, by whom it shall be forwarded to the Secretary of the Supreme Council.

The Cuba Five: Jeremiah O'Donovan Rossa, John Devoy, Henry Mulleda, John McClure and Charles Underwood O'Connell. (*Courtesy of the National Library of Ireland*)

On 11 July 1871 a Fenian assassination squad at Hardwicke Street, Dublin, shot retired RIC Head Constable Thomas Talbot. He was a figure of hatred as he had previously worked as a police informant against the Fenians. He died from his wounds on 17 July 1871. (*Courtesy of the National Library of Ireland*)

Robert Kelly was arrested following the shooting of Talbot. Refusing to surrender to the police, he was brought to the ground after a scuffle with three police officers. When arrested he gave the name Robert Pemberton.

Talbot lived for some hours after the shooting with a ball lodged in his spine. While his doctors fought over whether to extract the bullet or leave it where it was, Talbot died. By a clever piece of legal manoeuvring, Kelly's solicitor, Isaac Butt, put the onus of blame for Talbot's death on the doctors, thereby saving Kelly's life. Kelly was eventually imprisoned, but his acquittal for the killing itself saw calls for an abolition of trial by jury in Ireland. (*Courtesy of the National Library of Ireland*)

James Wilson   Michael Harrington

The conditional amnesty releasing Fenian prisoners did not apply to soldier Fenians, six of whom – Martin Hogan, James Wilson, Thomas Darragh, Robert Cranston, Thomas Hassett and Michael Harrington – were imprisoned at Freemantle in Western Australia. In 1871 Hogan smuggled a letter to John Devoy pleading for help, but nothing seems to have come of this. Three years later Wilson wrote to Devoy noting:

> Dear Friend, remember this is a voice from the tomb. For is not this a living tomb? In the tomb it is only a man's body that is good for worms, but in this living tomb the canker worm of care enters the very soul. That we have been nearly nine years in this living tomb since our first arrest and that it is impossible for mind or body to withstand the continual strain that is upon them. One or the other must give way. It is to aid us in this sad strait that I now, in the name of my comrades and myself, ask you to aid us ... we think if you forsake us, then we are friendless indeed.[1]

(*Courtesy of the New York Public Libraries*)

---

1   Ó Luing, Seán, *The Catalpa Rescue* (Tralee, 1965), p. 57.

Robert Cranston

Thomas Darragh

Martin Hogan

A ship was required to rescue the Freemantle prisoners, so Clan na Gael purchased a whaling vessel, the *Catalpa*, through James Reynolds, for $5,200. As part of the elaborate rescue mission, the ship was to be laden with cargo (to conceal its real purpose) and sail for Western Australia. It began its journey on 19 April 1875. (*Courtesy of Mercier Archive*)

John Breslin was a key figure in the escape plan. Originally from Drogheda, he had been sympathetic to Fenianism in the 1860s and had played a crucial part in the escape of James Stephens from Richmond Bridewell. Breslin had worked as a hospital steward within the prison. He used the duplicate keys made by Michael Lambert to open Stephens' cell and helped the Fenian leader scale the wall. For this he earned the nickname 'the Liberator'. It came as no surprise that Devoy was eager to use Breslin in the Freemantle escape plan and on 13 September 1875, with Fenian associate Tom Desmond, Breslin left San Francisco for Western Australia. Arriving on 16 November, he masqueraded as a wealthy American businessman named James Collins. Befriending the governor of Western Australia, he actually secured a tour of Freemantle Prison. Desmond posed as Tom Johnson, an Irish immigrant to Australia in search of work. The two contacted Edward Kelly and John King, two of the most powerful Fenians living in Australia, who provided them with money and assistance. Breslin eventually managed to get word of an escape plan to the Freemantle prisoners, setting the date for 17 April 1876. His message was incredibly simple – making his way to where James Wilson was working, near Freemantle jetty, Breslin whispered in his ear 'Monday morning'. (*Image from John Devoy,* Recollections of an Irish Rebel *(New York, 1929)*)

RESCUE OF THE
MILITARY FENIANS

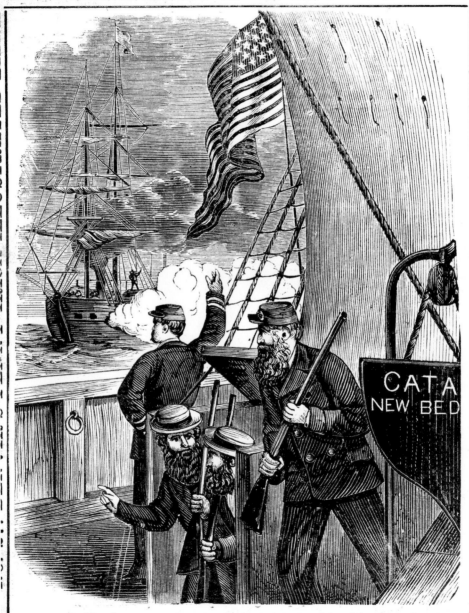

—" My flag protects me ; if you fire on this ship you fire on the American flag."—*Page* 23.

LIVERPOOL : JOHN DENVIR, 105, BYROM STREET.

82

On 17 April the *Catalpa* dropped anchor in international waters off Rockingham and dispatched a rowboat to the shore. As plans for the escape progressed, at 8.30 a.m. the six soldier Fenians – Hogan, Wilson, Darragh, Cranston, Hassett and Harrington – absconded from the prison and were met by John Breslin and Tom Desmond. Making their way to Rockingham they met George Smith Anthony, the captain of the *Catalpa*, who was waiting for them with the rowboat. Anthony, however, had been seen by a local man who was suspicious of him and alerted the police.

Boarding the rowboat, the men were trapped on the shoreline until dawn by an intense storm. By 7 a.m. the following morning, as the rowboat made for the *Catalpa*, they noticed the SS *Georgette* in the distance. This steamship had been commandeered by the colonial governor and was making for the *Catalpa*. In order to avoid drawing the attention of the *Georgette*, the men lay down in the rowboat. With tension palpable, the *Georgette* eventually ran out of fuel and was forced to withdraw to refuel, leaving the *Catalpa* unmolested. However, a police cutter with a crew of armed police was seen in the distance, so the fugitives raced to the *Catalpa* and boarded safely.

When the *Georgette* returned, heavily armed, its captain demanded the return of the prisoners and attempted to force the *Catalpa* out of international waters, firing a warning shot from its cannon. In a remarkably tense encounter, Captain Anthony raised the US flag and insisted to the *Georgette* that if they fired upon his vessel, they were firing upon the American flag in international waters – implying that the attack could be considered an act of war. Defeated, the *Georgette* returned to Australia as the *Catalpa* sailed towards freedom. Arriving in America on 21 August 1876, the Freemantle Six were greeted as heroes by Irish-Americans, their triumphal arrival marking one of the greatest successes in the history of Fenianism. (*Courtesy of Kilmainham Gaol Archive, 07PL-1C13-02*)

In 1877 Charles Stewart Parnell MP (*above*), of the Irish Parliamentary Party, met with the Fenian activist J. J. O'Kelly, who thought that Parnell was 'a man of promise' with whom the Clan could work to further the cause of Irish nationalism. On O'Kelly's recommendation Parnell met Dr William Carroll in Dublin and London the following year. He also met John Devoy twice in 1878, in Paris and Dublin. O'Kelly later recalled how:

> Parnell tried to convince us that we attached too little importance to the work that could be done in parliament if the right men were there to do it. He freely admitted that parliamentary work should only play a secondary part, and must be in conjunction with a movement in Ireland.[1]

(*Courtesy of the National Library of Ireland*)

---

1   J. J. O'Kelly to John Devoy, 5 August 1877, in O'Brien, William and Ryan, Desmond (eds), *Devoy's Post Bag*, Vol. 1 (Dublin, 1948), p. 59; *Irish Freedom*, December 1914, Kilmainham Gaol, Desmond l Museum 16NW-IK21-01.

Nationalists here will support you on the following conditions:

First—Abandonment of the federal demand and substitution of a general declaration in favor of self-government.

Second—Vigorous agitation of the land question on the basis of peasant proprietary, while accepting concessions tending to abolish arbitrary eviction.

Third—Exclusion of all sectarian issues from the platform.

Fourth—Irish members to vote together on all imperial and home questions, adopt an aggressive policy, and energetically resist coercive legislation.

Fifth—Advocacy of all struggling nationalities in the British empire and elsewhere.

On 12 October 1871 Parnell received a telegram from Irish-American nationalists inspired by John Devoy, saying that they would support him providing he gave a number of promises. It was hoped that a broad nationalist front could be established and Irish MPs would take their seats in Dublin, rather than London. Parnell made no formal response but took the opportunity to work with Irish-American Fenianism. (*Author's collection*)

Between 1876 and 1879 Ireland experienced the worst harvest on record since the famine. Many tenant farmers could not afford to pay rent to their landlords, and increasingly the prospect of starvation and eviction loomed on a scale not seen for forty years. Tenants' rights leagues emerged throughout the country, resulting in the formation of the Irish National Land League in October 1879. This signalled the start of a social revolution in Ireland between 1879 and 1882, known as the Land War. The Land War, a conflict of both violent and non-violent agitation, was fought between opposing forces of power and privilege on one side and the poor and marginalised on the other. Ultimately, it shifted the ownership of the land in Ireland from landlord to tenant. Many ordinary members of the IRB were heavily involved in the Land League, while Clan na Gael provided substantial funding to the organisation. Despite this, however, the IRB Supreme Council was hostile to the Land League, contending that it diverted nationalist Ireland from its real ambition – political independence. (*Courtesy of the National Library of Ireland*)

In 1875 Patrick Ford, the Irish-born owner of the New York-based *Irish World* newspaper, had suggested that he should set up a revolutionary fund to collect money for direct action in Britain. His idea was embraced by O'Donovan Rossa who, with Ford's help, established a skirmishing fund to finance transatlantic bombings. Writing of the fund, Ford commented:

We must take the offensive! Action gives life, action gives health. At present the Irish cause is received with a hiss and a sneer. This is telling against us. A few bold and devoted heroes must spring up and show the world there is still power in Fenianism not only to scare, but to hurt England.[1]

Thus the Fenians undertook a bombing campaign in Britain. Known as the Fenian dynamite campaign, it was financed by two groups within Irish America, Clan na Gael and the Skirmishers (a small splinter group centred around Jeremiah O'Donovan Rossa). (*Courtesy of the Library of Congress, LC–DIG–ggbain–06870*)

---

1   *The Irish World*, 4 December 1875.

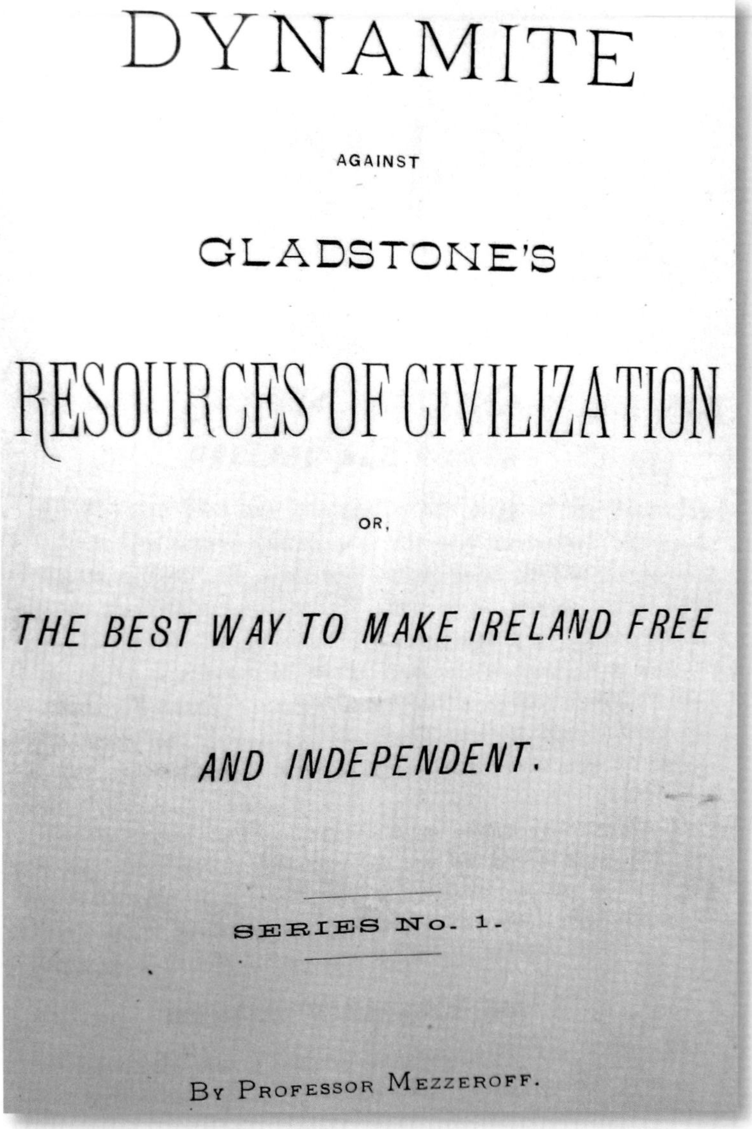

DYNAMITE

AGAINST

GLADSTONE'S

RESOURCES OF CIVILIZATION

OR,

THE BEST WAY TO MAKE IRELAND FREE

AND INDEPENDENT.

SERIES No. 1.

By Professor Mezzeroff.

A key element of the Skirmishers' strategy was the establishment of a dynamite school in Brooklyn to train Irishmen in the handling and use of explosives. An Irishman called Richard Rogers, who masqueraded as a Russian specialist named Professor Mezzeroff, ran the school. This pamphlet was written by Mezzeroff and is a succinct argument justifying a campaign of direct action in Britain utilising modern science. The title is a play on the words of British Prime Minister William Gladstone, who noted that the government would use the resources of civilisation to quell unrest in Ireland. (*Courtesy of the National Archives, London*)

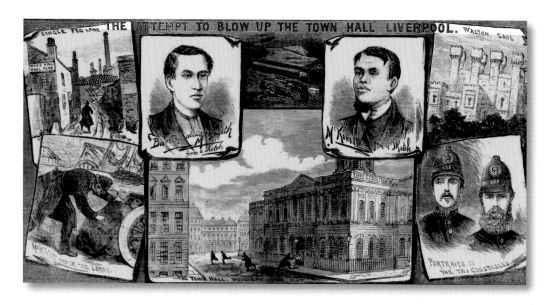

On 11 June 1881 Fenian dynamitards attempted to detonate a bomb on the steps of the entrance to Liverpool Town Hall. Disturbed by the police, they moved the bomb away from the building, but 'before they got more than five yards from it, it exploded'. The force of the blast was seen by onlookers, who recalled that 'the Town Hall windows … suffered severely from the broken fragments of iron piping, and the stonework in some places appeared as though it had been subjected to artillery'.[1] (*Courtesy of the National Library of Ireland*)

Robert Barton (alias James McGrath), one of the dynamitards at Liverpool Town Hall, was originally from County Derry, and worked as a quartermaster aboard a transatlantic steamer which greatly facilitated regular communications between America and Britain. (*Courtesy of Salford Police Museum*)

---

1   Liverpool constabulary force, central police office to the Lord Mayor of Liverpool, 10 June 1881, The National Archives, Kew, (TNA) HO 144/81/A5836; *The Annual Register: a review of public events at home and abroad for the year 1881* (London, 1882) p. 43; also Hansard debates, 11 June 1881 (London, 1881) col. 239.

James McKevitt, a native of Warrenpoint, County Down, was Barton's accomplice in the bombing. Arrested and interrogated by the police, McKevitt was contrite and co-operated with their investigations. Barton unhesitatingly told his questioners all he claimed to know of his involvement with Fenianism and explained how he had been manufacturing home-made explosives at his Liverpool home. He also said that his work was supervised by an Irish-American named Gleeson, who recruited and funded him with money raised from Irish-Americans, and was the head of a skirmishing cell sponsored by O'Donovan Rossa. Both men were sentenced to fifteen years in prison. (*Courtesy of Salford Police Museum*)

The Irish chief secretary was the representative of the British government's Irish policy in Westminster. Between 1880 and 1882 William Forster held the position. To deal with growing land agitation in Ireland, Forster introduced the Protection of Person and Property Act into parliament in January 1881. Becoming known as the 'Coercion Act', it gave the government sweeping powers – including detention without trial for any individual suspected of treasonable and agrarian offences. (*Author's collection*)

Above:
On 13 October 1881 Parnell was arrested and lodged in Kilmainham Gaol, charged with sedition. His imprisonment was facilitated by the Coercion Act. (*Courtesy of the National Library of Ireland*)

Overleaf:
On 18 October 1881 the Kilmainham prisoners issued the No Rent manifesto, calling on tenant farmers not to pay rent to their landlords, to avoid the land courts and to hold the harvest. Within two days the Land League was outlawed. (*Courtesy of the National Library of Ireland*)

NO RENT!

NO LANDLORDS GRASSLAND

Tenant Farmers, now is the time. Now is the hour.
You proved false to the first call made upon you.
REDEEM YOUR CHARACTER NOW

NO RENT

UNTIL THE SUSPECTS ARE RELEASED

The man who pays Rent (whether an abatement
is offered or not) while PARNELL DILLON &c.
are in Jail, will be looked upon as a Traitor to his
Country and a disgrace to his class

No RENT, No Compromise, No Landlords' Grassland,
Under any circumstances.

Avoid the Police, and listen not to spying and delu-
ding Bailiffs

NO RENT! LET THE LANDTHIEVES DO THEIR WORST!

THE LAND FOR THE PEOPLE!

As a growing response to the crisis in Ireland, in the autumn of 1881 a three-man committee was established. Although few details are known about this committee, it is known that it included Frank Byrne, the secretary of the Land League of Great Britain (*right*). The committee wanted to establish an assassination squad within Fenianism and sent IRB activist John Walsh to Dublin to make contact with Fenian activists. (*Author's collection*)

One of Walsh's first recruits into the assassination squad was Edward McCaffrey, a van driver and veteran of the Fenian conspiracy in Dublin, who lived at 21 Peter Street. McCaffrey was an inspired choice as he had contacts with Fenian centres throughout the capital. (*Courtesy of the National Library of Ireland*)

Through McCaffrey, Walsh was introduced to James Carey, a prominent Dublin Republican and member of a vigilance committee dedicated to rooting out informers. Walsh told Carey that he wanted to establish an assassination society that would 'make history'. Carey joined him in what was to become known as the Irish National Invincibles.[1] (*Courtesy of the National Library of Ireland*)

---

1   The evidence of James Carey before John Adye Curran, Kilmainham Gaol, Dublin, 2 March 1883, TNA HO 144/98/A25908C.

The Invincibles' oath, here handwritten by Patrick Sheridan, starts with the line: 'I _____ of my own volition do solemnly swear hereon and hereby that I will do my utmost to establish the National Independence of Ireland and to bear true allegiance to the organisation of the Irish Invincibles and implicitly obey my superior officers.' (*Courtesy of Tim Sheridan*)

Patrick J. Sheridan joined the IRB while living in Northern England, and took part in the abortive Chester Castle raid. He was sent by Frank Byrne to Ireland to help organise the assassination society and met with James Carey. (*Author's collection*)

Captain John McCafferty, who had also taken part in the Chester Castle raid, was to act as a go-between, shuffling money and orders from Byrne to the Dublin Directory, the governing body of the Invincibles. He made regular trips to Britain, Ireland and France, and on several occasions met with Carey, supplying him with money to advance the aims of the Directory. McCafferty favoured the use of knives, recommending the tying of cord around their handles so as to secure a better grip. (*Courtesy of the National Library of Ireland*)

Finally Byrne dispatched Patrick Joseph Tynan to Dublin to coordinate the activity of the Dublin Invincibles. Tynan gained notoriety with the supposed title of No. 1 (director) of the Invincible conspiracy, but No. 1 was actually a reference to a photograph of Tynan produced during a later cross-examination of James Carey. In 1894 he wrote a rather sensationalised version of his memoirs, entitled *The Irish National Invincibles and their Times*. (*Image taken from* The Irish National Invincibles and their Times *(London, 1894)*)

James Mullet, a publican and a hard-line Fenian, became the chairman of the Dublin Directory of the Invincibles. He was arrested in February 1882 as part of government inquiries into the assassination of a Fenian informant, Bernard Bailey, at Skippers Alley, Dublin, earlier that month. (*Courtesy of the National Library of Ireland*)

James Mullet's arrest forced a change within the command structure of the Invincibles and he was replaced as chairman by Edward McCaffrey. In the aftermath of the Invincible conspiracy he was sentenced to ten years' imprisonment. Daniel Curley (*above*) replaced McCaffrey as chairman. Curley was a natural choice – he was centre of a Fenian circle – and recruited several figures into the conspiracy, including Joe Brady and Michael Fagan, both of whom were executed in April 1883. (*Courtesy of the National Library of Ireland*)

On 2 May 1882 Parnell was released from Kilmainham Gaol under the terms of the so-called Kilmainham Treaty. While there was no actual treaty written down, it was verbally understood that Parnell would use his influence to quell violence and conspiracy, and the government would cease coercion. (*Author's collection*)

William Forster was horrified by the release of Parnell and resigned as Irish chief secretary. Lord Frederick Cavendish (*right*), who arrived in Ireland on 6 May 1882, replaced him. Thomas Henry Burke (*left*), the under-secretary at Dublin Castle, was the most senior civil servant in Ireland and responsible for the daily administration of Castle bureaucracy. (*Courtesy of the National Library of Ireland*)

On 6 May 1882 Cavendish and Burke were assassinated while walking in the Phoenix Park, Dublin. Later that evening the assassins left a card into all the major newspapers in Dublin identifying themselves as members of the Irish National Invincibles. (*Courtesy of the National Library of Ireland*)

On 9 May 1882 Thomas Henry Burke was laid to rest beside his father under a Celtic cross in Glasnevin Cemetery, Dublin. The ornamental carved-stone cover of the grave bears the inscription, 'Sacred to the memory of Thomas Henry Burke Esq. who was murdered in the Phoenix Park May 6th 1882. He pleased God and was beloved'. His friends erected a second memorial adjacent reading 'To the memory of Thomas Henry Burke, Under Secretary to the Lord Lieutenant of Ireland. Assassinated in the Phoenix Park. This monument is erected by his many friends among the Irish Resident Magistrates as a mark of their appreciation of his high character and eminent public service. RIP'. Burke is the only man in Glasnevin Cemetery with two monuments. (*Courtesy of Glasnevin Cemetery*)

Following the assassinations, Dublin Castle established a permanent secret service department called the Office of Assistant Under-secretary for Police and Crime. Henry Brackenbury, a career soldier, was appointed to head the new department on 25 May 1882, but was not in the position for long. (*Image from Henry Brackenbury,* Some Memories of My Spare Time *(1909)*)

Edward George Jenkinson was chosen as Brackenbury's replacement. He established a wide-ranging, intelligence-led, counter-Fenian strategy, employing an army of spies, agent provocateurs and informers, often with a disregard for the established rule of law. (*Courtesy of Getty images*)

Inspector John Mallon was a detective in the 'G' Division of the Dublin Metropolitan Police. Having an extensive informer network, he claimed to know who had assassinated Cavendish and Burke within two weeks of their death. He was hampered by a lack of solid evidence, however, and the Invincibles remained at large. (*Image taken from Frederick Moir Bussy,* Irish Conspiracies: Recollections of John Mallon *(London, 1910)*)

In order to defeat the Invincibles, a Star Chamber of Inquiry was established. This provided for a magistrate to have the power to summon a suspected individual for interrogation under oath without legal representation. John Adye Curran, a police magistrate, was chosen to head the inquiry. With Mallon's assistance he interviewed leading Fenians, including twenty-six Invincibles. (*Image taken from John Adye Curran,* Reminiscences of John Adye Curran *(London, 1914)*)

Robert Farrell had been an active Fenian since 1876. Although he was not in the Phoenix Park at the time of the killings, he was an Invincible and was arrested by Mallon. Brought before the inquiry, he disclosed all that he knew and signed a statement implicating several Invincibles in the conspiracy. (*Courtesy of the National Library of Ireland*)

Twenty-six Invincibles were arrested and placed in Kilmainham Gaol. They were tried at the crown magistrate's court, Kilmainham, in February 1883. All claimed their innocence and denied the legitimacy of the court. The lithograph shows some of the prisoners in the dock. (*Courtesy of the National Library of Ireland*)

James Fitzharris was a Dublin cabdriver known as 'Skin the Goat'. A committed Invincible, he drove a cab to the Phoenix Park on 6 May and assisted in the escape of several Invincibles following the assassinations. One of the twenty-six men arrested, he was picked up at his home at 15 Brady's Cottage, Lime Street, Dublin, on 6 February 1883. Tried for murder, he was found not guilty, but was retried and found guilty of being an accessory to the assassination. For this he was sentenced to life imprisonment. Offered a reward of £10,000 to inform, Fitzharris refused to turn on his comrades. In 1898 his wife Kate died and the IRB took care of her funeral arrangements, with Maud Gonne laying a wreath on her grave in deference to her husband's sacrifice. Fitzharris was released in 1899. (*Courtesy of Glasnevin Museum*)

Myles Kavanagh (*left*) and Peter Carey (*right*), James Carey's brother, were tricked into revealing details of the Invincibles' conspiracy. Leaving them alone in the infirmary, Inspector Mallon hid behind an oak vent, listening and taking notes. Mallon then convinced Kavanagh that he knew the intricacies of the conspiracy, and that James Fitzharris, who detested Kavanagh, had told him everything he needed to know, making Kavanagh's execution inevitable. Both Kavanagh and Carey turned crown's evidence against their former confederates and both were sent to Australia with new identities. (*Courtesy of the National Library of Ireland*)

James Carey was tricked into believing that Daniel Curley was giving evidence against him. As he languished in his empty prison cell, an incessant psychological warfare was practised against him. Carey was unveiled as a crown witness on 19 February (*above*) and gave extensive details of the conspiracy. (*Courtesy of the National Library of Ireland*)

Joe Brady was tried and found guilty of the assassinations on 11 April 1883 at Green Street Courthouse, Dublin. He had been the assassin of Burke, and he also cut Cavendish's throat shortly afterwards to make sure he was dead. He was executed at Kilmainham Gaol on 14 May 1883. After his execution, he was beheaded and his brain was sent to be dissected and studied by craniologists at the Royal College of Surgeons in Dublin. (*Courtesy of the National Library of Ireland*)

Daniel Curley appeared at Green Street Courthouse on 16 April 1883. Sentenced to be hanged, Curley made a powerful speech, concluding that he would take the secrets of the Invincible conspiracy to his grave:

> I was let into a number of their secrets, and I will say here today that I will bring them to my grave faithfully and truly; and as to my own life, if I had a thousand lives to lose, I would rather lose them sooner than bring to my grave the name of informer and that I should save my life by betraying my fellow man … I am a member of the Invincible society – undoubtedly, unhesitatingly.[1]

Curley was executed at Kilmainham Gaol on 18 May 1883. (*Courtesy of the National Library of Ireland*)

---

1   *The Freeman's Journal*, 19 April 1883; *The Irish Times*, 3 May 1883.

Originally from Westmeath, Michael Fagan was twenty-four years of age when he was arrested. He was illiterate and lived in Dublin's Buckingham Street. He was a leading figure within Dublin Fenianism and had acted as centre of a Fenian circle previously. On the day of the assassinations, Fagan was lying in wait for Thomas Henry Burke in the Phoenix Park and witnessed the killing of Burke and Cavendish. Michael Fagan was executed in Kilmainham Gaol on 28 May 1883. (*Courtesy of the National Library of Ireland*)

On 2 May 1883, at Green Street Courthouse, Thomas Caffery's trial took less than an hour. Appearing in the dock he admitted his involvement in the conspiracy and his presence in the Phoenix Park on 6 May 1882, stating:

> My Lord I have to say, standing here on the brink of my grave, that I did not know what was going to happen twenty minutes or half an hour before, I was ordered to go there and if I did not go there my life would have been taken. That is all I have to say my Lord.

The only one of the five executed to plead guilty, Caffery was hanged at Kilmainham on 2 June 1883. (*Courtesy of the National Library of Ireland*)

Timothy Kelly was tried three times for the assassinations of Cavendish and Burke. Found guilty on the third occasion, he was executed at Kilmainham on 9 June 1883. At nineteen years of age he was the youngest of the Invincibles to be hanged. On the night before his execution Kelly is reputed to have sung *Salve Regina* and *The Memory of the Past*. (*Courtesy of the National Library of Ireland*)

The Hanlon Brothers were part of the Invincible party waiting for Burke. Joseph Hanlon (*below*) turned informer and offered evidence against Kelly. For this he was given a new identity and resettled in Australia. His brother, Lawrence (*left*), who refused to give evidence, was sentenced to life imprisonment. (*Courtesy of the National Library of Ireland*)

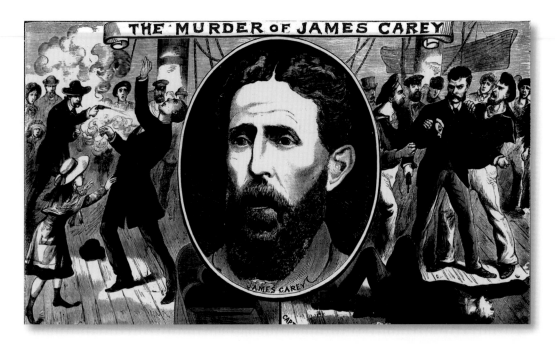

THE MURDER OF JAMES CAREY

JAMES CAREY

As part of the deal reached with James Carey in return for his information, he was to be given a new life outside Ireland. Inspector John Mallon collected Carey from Kilmainham Gaol and took him to Dublin Castle where he gave Carey a revolver and some money, to be used for protection and the building of a new life in the colonies.

Carey travelled first to England, where he was reunited with his family. Carey's wife, Maggie, had brought the family to London, where they were disguised as an immigrant Irish family in the East End. Two days later, on 3 July, with Carey using the pseudonym James Power, he and his family were put on the *Kinfaun's Castle*, a steamer bound for the Cape of Good Hope.

By coincidence, also on board was an Irishman, Patrick O'Donnell. O'Donnell was born in Gweedore, County Donegal in 1835, and was sailing on the *Kinfaun's Castle* to make his fortune in South Africa. As a fellow Irishman, O'Donnell met and befriended Carey. On learning that O'Donnell was going to Cape Town, Carey persuaded him to follow him on to Natal.

While in Cape Town, O'Donnell discovered Carey's true identity and planned to expose him rather than kill him. With the Careys, O'Donnell boarded another boat, *The Melrose*, bound for Natal. Arranging a meeting with Carey in the ship's bar, O'Donnell denounced him as an informer and exposed him as James Carey. Carey sprang to his feet immediately, reaching for his pistol to kill O'Donnell. O'Donnell was too fast, however, and drew his pistol on Carey, shooting him three times and killing him. (*Courtesy of the National Library of Ireland*)

A page from *The Weekly Freeman* of 23 July 1883 about the James Carey assassination. (*Courtesy of the National Library of Ireland*)

Patrick O'Donnell was deported to London and tried for the assassination of James Carey in the Old Bailey Courthouse from 30 November to 1 December 1883. He was found guilty of 'wilful murder' and hanged at Newgate Gaol, London, on 17 December 1883. (*Author's collection*)

Just a day after O'Donnell's execution, Joe Poole was executed at Richmond Bridewell. Originally arrested on a charge of conspiracy relating to the Phoenix Park assassinations, Poole was acquitted of the charge, but re-arrested immediately for the killing of the informer John Kenny. (*Courtesy of the National Library of Ireland*)

William Lamie, Poole's brother-in-law, gave evidence against him during his trial. He had earlier been a witness in the trials of the Invincibles and claimed that Poole had spoken to him about the killing of Kenny. In his testimony, Lamie said that Poole had complained that the daggers that killed Kenny were blunt and 'like chisels'. (*Courtesy of the National Library of Ireland*)

Red Jim McDermott was an agent provocateur employed by the head of the secret service, Edward George Jenkinson. He was responsible for the arrest of several Fenian conspirators between March and April 1883. McDermott was also part of the Fenian conspiracy which planned simultaneous bombings in Britain and Ireland. Through McDermott, the Fenian conspiracy was unknowingly funded by the secret service fund in London. He was one of the most notorious British agents of the late nineteenth century and when he was exposed his infamy rivalled that of James Carey. Escaping from Ireland, McDermott was followed by an IRB activist, William Riordan, who, on meeting him at Le Havre, drugged and interrogated him. However, McDermott escaped and made for Canada. He was lured to America by O'Donovan Rossa, where he was shot by two Fenian assassins in Ryan's Saloon in New York, but survived and escaped. Returning to England he was arrested in August 1883 and tried for conspiracy. With his case collapsing due to a lack of evidence, he was quietly shuffled out of England to Europe, where he eventually settled in France. (*Author's collection*)

Dr Thomas Gallagher was the head of a Clan na Gael bombing cell. Using the alias of 'Mr Fletcher' he arrived in Britain in March 1883. He was arrested the following month but developed acute insanity while a prisoner and was released on medical grounds in 1896. (*Courtesy of the National Library of Ireland*)

The first signatory to the Easter Proclamation of 1916, Thomas James Clarke was arrested on 4 April 1883 in possession of several bags of nitro-glycerine explosive at 17 Nelson Square, London. He had been involved in the Irish-American bombing cell headed by Dr Gallagher. Sentenced to life imprisonment, Clarke was the last dynamitard to be released from prison in 1898. (*Courtesy of the National Library of Ireland*)

James J. Murphy (alias Alfred White-head) was Dr Gallagher's deputy and established a paint shop in Birmingham as a front operation to facilitate the purchase of materials necessary for the production of explosives. Arrested after an extensive police surveillance operation on 4 April 1883, he was sentenced to life imprisonment. Like Gallagher, in jail he experienced immense mental strain and developed insanity. (*Author's collection*)

John O'Connor (alias Henry Dalton) was an active dynamitard who had been trained in the handling and use of explosives in the Brooklyn dynamite school. Arriving in Britain in the spring of 1883, he worked with Glasgow Fenians, training men in the use of explosives. Duped by Red Jim McDermott, Dalton was involved in a phoney conspiracy as McDermott's accomplice. Arrested in April 1883, he was sentenced to life imprisonment. (*Courtesy of the National Library of Ireland*)

On 30 October 1883 there were two explosions on the London Underground, at Praed Street and Charing Cross. The dynamitards threw bombs from the moving carriages as they exited tunnels near the train platforms. The public were thrown into confusion and panic.

At Praed Street, seventy-two people were injured in the bombing. Within minutes a bomb also exploded in a tunnel at Charing Cross Station. The startled public at Charing Cross initially believed that the blast was the result of an accidental gas explosion, but on hearing of the first blast in Praed Street, they soon realised that something more serious was occurring.

Following the bombings there was a marked decline in the value of Metropolitan Railway shares by half a percentage point in its district service, and seventeen and half percent in its parent company on the London Stock Exchange, along with a marked decrease in general confidence, which depressed the market. (*Author's collection*)

On 26 February 1884 a Fenian bomb detonated in the cloakroom of Victoria Station in London. Several more explosives, which had failed to detonate, were discovered at the Charing Cross, Paddington and Ludgate Hill railway termini. Despite the failure of the conspiracy to bomb four train stations in London city centre, it was apparent to all that, as one newspaper commented, 'the entire plot had been defused by "a hair's breath".'[1] The general public were terrified and 'as February went out London absolutely trembled at the sight of each black valise – in Railway Stations and Railway Trains, people instinctively edged away from every Gladstone Bag – in Tramcars and Buses, suspicious looks were bestowed by old ladies on the most innocent portmanteau'.[2] (*Courtesy of the National Library of Ireland*)

Opposite:
Fenian bombs and shrapnel discovered following the attempted explosion at Ludgate Hill, London. Note the use of the term IRA (Irish Republican Army). (*Courtesy of the Metropolitan Police London*)

---

1   *The Chronicle*, 27 February 1884, London Metropolitan Archive ACC/1297/MET/10/038/001.
2   *The Penny Illustrated Pape*r, 8 March 1884.

An artist's impression of the Fenian bombs in *The Graphic*, 8 March 1884.

Image 1: Mechanism
- (A)   The Pistol.
- (B)   The Revolving Winder.
- (C)   The Trigger.
- (D)   The Hammer.
- (E)   The Pistol Barrel.

Image 2: The cake of dynamite (6 inches by 3 inches by ½ inch)
- (A)   Holes in which the detonators were placed.
- (B)   Place of the paper covering, bearing the words 'Atlas Powder A' – this was torn away.

Image 3: Combined cap and cartridge for pistol.
- (A)   The end of the cartridge showing the indentation caused by the fall of the hammer.

Image 4: The detonator containing fulminate of mercury.

Image 5: The fuse spring discovered at Victoria Station.

Image 6: The cash box discovered at Paddington Station which contained the dynamite and the bomb described as an 'infernal machine'.

Image 7: The leather bag containing the cash box.
- (A)   The box wrapped in cloth on either side of which a sizable quantity of dynamite was placed.

(Courtesy of the National Library of Ireland)

In March 1883, as a result of the Fenian bombings in Britain, a plain-clothes detective department called the Special Irish Branch was established. Its purpose was to monitor the activities of the Irish community in Britain and suspected Fenian conspirators. It was made up of Irishmen serving within the London Metropolitan Police, as it was decided they would draw less attention in undercover activities, and its headquarters were in Scotland Yard, with the offices located above a public toilet. In May 1884 Fenian dynamitards planted a bomb in the toilet, destroying the headquarters. This is a photograph of the damage caused by the Fenian bomb: note the Rising Sun Saloon on the left, which was totally wrecked by the impact. (*Courtesy of the National Library of Ireland*)

Born in 1845 John Daly was a veteran Fenian and fought in the 1867 rebellion. In 1884 he was arrested at Birkenhead railway station and found to be in the possession of grenades. It was asserted that he had intended to use these to assassinate the government. A confederate, Big Dan O'Neill, who actually worked for British intelligence, had given him the bombs. British intelligence regarded Daly as 'the most bloody-minded fanatic since the days of Guy Fawkes'.[1] Found guilty of treason felony, Daly was sentenced to life imprisonment, but was released on 16 August 1896.

Following his release, Daly was active in Fenian politics and the amnesty campaign seeking the release of the imprisoned dynamitards from British jails. In 1900 and again in 1901 he was elected mayor of Limerick city, and remained a thorn in the side of the British administration of Ireland, awarding the freedom of the city to several declared enemies of the British state, including Paul Kruger, the president of the Transvaal during the Boer War, and Thomas Clarke. Daly was certainly aware of the plans for the Easter Rising of 1916, a rebellion after which his nephew, Edward Daly, and friend, Thomas Clarke, were executed at Kilmainham Gaol. Badly affected by the executions and in continuous poor health, John Daly died in Limerick on 16 June 1916. (*Courtesy of the National Library of Ireland*)

---

1   Reference: Nicholas Gosselin to Henry Matthews, Secretary of State for the Home Department, 28 August 1891, TNA HO 144/193A/A6664B.

Known as 'The Little Captain', William Mackey Lomasney was a central figure in Clan na Gael and was involved in several Clan bombing operations in 1884. Lomasney, John Fleming and his brother-in-law Peter Mallon, were involved in an attempt to destroy the London bridge network and plunge the city into chaos. (*Courtesy of the National Library of Ireland*)

On the evening of 13 December 1884 Lomasney, Mallon and Fleming's first target was London Bridge. Some minutes before 6 p.m., the dynamitards rowed underneath its dark granite structure. Lomasney had set the fuse, but as they prepared to set sail to the next bridge, the bomb exploded prematurely. What followed was recorded as 'a tremendous report'. This lithograph is an interpretation of the explosion taken from *The Graphic* newspaper. (*Courtesy of the National Library of Ireland*)

THE TOWER OF LONDON, FROM THE THAMES RIVER.

On 24 January 1885 Fenian dynamitards detonated simultaneous bombs at the Tower of London and in the chamber of the House of Commons. Innumerable newspapers recalled a scene of shattered windows, seats ripped asunder and covered in layers of dust, and reported a chamber filled with the smell of dynamite. The force of the blast had separated the national shield engraved with the Irish harp which hung under a sculpture of the crown indicating imperial possessions. It fell near the chair of the Sergeant-at-Arms. In reporting this, the irony was not lost to anyone: the Fenian bomber had separated Ireland from the British crown. This day became known as Dynamite Saturday.[1] (*Courtesy of the National Library of Ireland*)

---

1   Sullivan, T. D., *Recollections of Troubled Times in Irish Politics* (Dublin, 1905), p. 172; see also Edward Walter Hamilton, 24 January 1885 in Bahlman, Dudley (ed.), *The Diary of Sir Edward Walter Hamilton* (Oxford, 1972), p. 779.

James Gilbert Cunningham was the Tower of London dynamitard. He entered the Tower with explosives strapped to his body underneath his overcoat. In the aftermath of the blast, Inspector Abberline of the London Metropolitan Police ordered the Tower locked down, insisting that no one was to leave until they had been questioned as to their business inside the building. Cunningham was trapped in the Tower when the gates were shut. Interviewed by a police panel, Cunningham provided a false name, James George Gilbert, and claimed to be an English labourer, previously working at Liverpool. Abberline asked Cunningham several questions as to his business in the Tower, to which he hesitantly responded. This hesitation would have been understandable, given he had just been caught up in an explosion, yet Abberline was interested by Cunningham's obvious Irish-American accent during a time of heightened vigilance regarding Irish-American strangers, and recommended further questioning. Following this, there was little doubt as to his involvement in the explosion.

Two women were badly wounded in the Tower bombing. The first was Elizabeth Ballam, whose face was lacerated by flying glass and who developed permanent deafness. Ann Nunn received burns to her face and body. Two boys were also hurt – Herbert George in the thighs and hands, and Ernest Stratton, who was cut in the head by glass. Both were carried out of the fire by the police. Cunningham was sentenced to life imprisonment. (*Courtesy of the National Library of Ireland*)

Recognising the growing influence of the Irish Parliamentary Party in parliament and the potential of Fenian bombings undermining their work, Clan na Gael issued a private circular informing members that 'the dynamite operations so far conducted have compelled the enemy to recognise the constitutional party, and we are now in a fair way to reap the benefits and results of the heroic work of the members … We expect to resume active operations after the present exigencies of the constitutional party are

ARLIAMENTARY · PARTY · OF · 1885.

Printed by FORSTER & CO., Ltd., DUBLIN.

passed.' This circular clearly indicates that the dynamite campaign was perceived as a potential threat to the success of the Irish Party in the forthcoming 1885 general election, where the party hoped to increase its representation in parliament. Against this background it was decided by the Clan's leadership to give the politicians a chance, and constitutional nationalists nearly secured the balance of power in parliament, returning eighty-six members. (*Courtesy of the National Library of Ireland*)

Following the 1885 election, the leader of the Liberal Party, William Ewart Gladstone, made serious overtures to the Irish Parliamentary Party on the issue of Irish Home Rule. With Irish Party support, Gladstone became prime minister on 1 February 1886 and was intent on introducing an Irish Home Rule Bill. This poster, which is clearly from an opponent of Home Rule, captures the unlikely alliance and represents the idea that Home Rule will lead to Gladstone's downfall. Parnell's horse has a headband with the word 'Dynamiter' on it, an attempt to connect him to Fenianism. (*Courtesy of Patrick Mulvany*)

HOUSE OF COMMONS

SUSPENSE !!!

On 8 April 1886, Gladstone presented the Home Rule Bill to the British parliament, with a plan for a two-tiered Irish parliament in Dublin. This would consist of a House of Lords, comprising 103 members elected by landlords and the aristocracy, and a House of Commons, comprising 204 members elected by the general Irish electorate. The bill was defeated by 341 votes to 311. Gladstone immediately resigned as prime minister, calling a general election for 1886. In this poster, Ireland waits in suspense for the outcome of the vote as the election is fought for the first time on the Irish question. The British electorate chose to support the Conservatives, who opposed Home Rule, and on 25 July 1886 the Marquis of Salisbury was elected prime minister. For the next six years Britain had a stable Conservative government, committed to the maintenance of the Union at all costs. (*Courtesy of the National Library of Ireland*)

During Queen Victoria's jubilee year of 1887, which is celebrated in the unusual picture above from a graphic newspaper called the *St Stephens Review*, opponents of Home Rule hoped to discredit the Irish Parliamentary Party by associating it with an alleged Fenian conspiracy to assassinate the Queen. General Francis Millen (*right*), a leading Fenian and British agent since the 1860s, was central to the British government's attempts to pin such a plot on the Fenians. Through Millen, letters were posted to several Irish MPs in London, one of whom, Joseph Nolan, made contact with Millen's daughters and two Fenian dynamitards. These letters were signed by Millen who was under surveillance at Boulogne, France. (*Courtesy of the National Library of Ireland*)

Michael Harkins and Thomas Callan were arrested for their involvement in the alleged plot. They had been associated with Joseph Moroney (alias Joseph Melville), who, through Francis Millen, was in contact with the Irish Parliamentary Party. Another man who was implicated in the plot, Joseph Cohen, died of tuberculosis in London. This image, taken from the *Penny Illustrated Paper*, shows some of the alleged conspirators: Melville dining in a London restaurant with his lover Miss Kennedy and the dynamitards Cohen and Harkins. (*Courtesy of Patrick Mulvany*)

The jubilee plot came to nothing. Had it succeeded, Millen's letters would have implicated the Irish Parliamentary Party in the outrage, Parnell would have been discredited and fatally undermined, and his party annihilated. Home Rule as a policy would never have been resurrected and Ireland's place would have been consolidated within the United Kingdom. Something else was now needed to connect the parliamentarians with the dynamitards, and efforts to associate Parnellism with Fenian conspirators continued unabated. One example is this poster, which portrays Parnell as a king, sitting on a throne adorned by weapons and the skulls of Cavendish and Burke, the two men assassinated in the Phoenix Park in 1882. (*Courtesy of Aidan Lambert*)

Sir Robert Anderson was born in Dublin in 1841 and later graduated from Trinity College Dublin. Following the Fenian crisis of the 1860s, he was briefly involved in a counter-Fenian unit established at Scotland Yard. An expert on the Fenians, Anderson was both Brackenbury's and Jenkinson's London representative at the Home Office. He was a determined opponent of Parnellism and actively sought to publish a connection between the Irish Parliamentary Party and the Fenians. Anderson privately supplied *The Times* with a wealth of materials linking Parnellism to Fenian conspiracies and provided the basis for a series of articles entitled 'Parnellism and Crime' first published on 7 March 1887, which sought 'to remind the public of certain facts connected with the Home Rule agitation in Ireland which are too often permitted to drop out of sight.'[1] Supporting this sensationalist narrative, *The Times* bombastically claimed that the Irish Parliamentary Party were complicit with Fenian conspirators, alleging:

> Murderers provide their funds, murderers share their inmost counsels, murderers have gone forth from the league offices to set their bloody work afoot, and have presently returned to consult the 'constitutional leaders' on the advancement of the cause.[2]

(*Image from Robert Anderson,* Sidelights on the Home Rule Movement *(London, 1906)*)

---

1 Anon, *Parnellism and Crime*: reprinted from *The Times,* revised edition (London, 1887), p. 29.
2 *Ibid.*, p. 9.

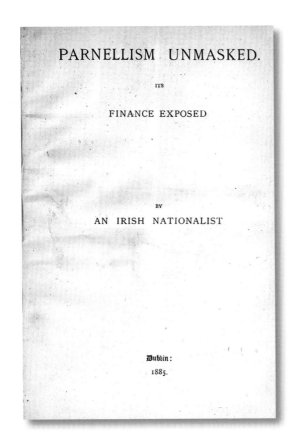

PARNELLISM UNMASKED.

ITS

FINANCE EXPOSED

BY

AN IRISH NATIONALIST

Dublin:
1885.

In 1885, sometime nationalist and Dublin journalist Richard Pigott wrote *Parnellism Unmasked*, a sensationalised exposé of the relationship between Parnellism and Fenianism. In 1886 he forged letters purporting to come from various members of the Fenians, which he claimed associated Parnell with the Phoenix Park assassinations. *The Times* published the letters on 18 April 1887. (*Courtesy of the National Library of Ireland*)

Opposite:
This forged letter, supposedly from Parnell, was published by *The Times* on 18 April 1887.

I am not surprised at your friend's anger but he and you should know that to denounce the murders was the only course open to us. To do that promptly was plainly our best policy.

But you can tell him and all others concerned that though I regret the accident of Lord F. Cavendish's death I cannot refuse to admit that Burke got no more than his deserts.

You are at liberty to show him this, and others whom you can trust also, but let not my address be known. He can write to House of Commons.

(*Author's collection*)

15/5/82

Dear Sir,

I am not surprised at your friend's anger but he and you should know that to denounce the murders was the only course open to us. To do that promptly was plainly ~~the only~~ ~~course~~ our best policy.

But you can tell him and all others concerned that though I regret the accident of Lord F Cavendish's death I cannot refuse to admit that Burke got no more than his deserts

You are at liberty to show this him, and others whom you can trust also, but let not my address be known. He can write to House of Commons

Yours very truly
Chas. S Parnell

Mr. John Morley and   Mr. Henry Labouchere talk it over

The letters are submitted to Pigott, and he swears that they are in Mr. Parnell's hand-writing

Pigott : " Mr. Lewis assumed his severest manner. He sat on a chair and denounced me at once as a forger "

Sir Charles Russell : " Do you feel ashamed of yourself ?" — ' I do not.' Sir Charles : " You do not ?" — " I do not, sir, and it is scandalous to be so questioned. I affirm distinctly——" The President : " But, witness, we are the judges, irrespective of how counsel proceed."—Witness, (turning to the Judges) : " I beg pardon, my lord. What I say is, I think I ought to be allowed to say at once that I utterly deny that I forged these letters." The President : " Very well."—Witness (continuing) : " And that if I did so I should not be here." Sir Charles : " Not if you could help it." (Laughter).—Witness : " Why could I not help it ?" — " You will hear presently, I think, Mr. Pigott."

Mr. T. Wemyss Reid produces photographs of Pigott's correspondence with Mr. W. E. Forster

" Litera scripta manet "—The fatal pen : Sir Charles Russell : " Supposing you wanted to forge a document, would it be at all any help to you to have a genuine letter before you ?"—Pigott : " Of course it would. There is no doubt about that." " How should you use it ?"—" I should copy it, of course." " How would you proceed ?"—" I can't say." " Just give us your best idea ?"—" I don't pretend to any experience in that line." (Laughter) " What I mean is, just see how you would begin if you were called upon to forge a document ?"—" I cannot do anything of the kind." " Theoretically ?"—" I do not see any use in discussing theories." " Let me suggest to you. Would you, for instance, put delicate tissue-paper over it and trace it ?"—" Yes." "But how would you proceed then ?" (Laughter). " Oh, I don't know." (Laughter). " Supposing you had a genuine letter and you wanted to forge it, a delicate tissue-paper placed over it would at all events enable you to trace the characters ?"—" That is the way you would probably do it." " But how would you ?"—" I fancy I would trust myself to imitation."

Pigott confronted with his letters to Archbishop Walsh. Sir Charles Russell : " Now, Mr. Pigott, pull yourself together "

Dr. A. Commins, Member for Roscommon (South)

Bryce, M.P., falls asleep on the bench ; Mr. Justice Day lets fall all the photographs of the letters and wakes him

140

Addressing *The Times'* allegations of Parnellite complicity with conspiracy, the British government established a special commission to investigate the nature of the claims and to provide legal justification for the accusations. Rather than act as a commission of balanced inquiry, the Special Commission was weighted against the Irish Parliamentary Party, who wished to secure a definitive vindication of *The Times'* allegations.

The commission lasted for eight months, with over 128 public sessions, and interviewed over 450 witnesses in what was a significant legal undertaking. The image opposite shows the cross-examination of Richard Pigott by the commission. Despite the speculation and public interest in the commission, the inquiry was at times lacklustre. Wading through the evidence of hundreds of tenant farmers, members of the Land League, former Fenian activists, politicians, police officers, justices of the peace, landlords and gombeen men to list a few, the commission began an extensive investigation of Irish nationalist activity and *The Times'* accusations, opening on 22 October 1888. Its most famous witness was Henri Le Caron. (*Courtesy of the National Library of Ireland*)

Henri Le Caron was the alias used by Englishman Thomas Miller Beech. He was involved with Fenianism for twenty-five years and was sensationally exposed as a British agent at the Special Commission when he gave evidence against Parnell. Making a direct association with the Irish Parliamentary Party leader, he asserted that Parnell had told him, 'there need be no misunderstanding. We are working for a common purpose – for the independence of Ireland, just as you are doing; I have long ceased to believe that anything but force of arms will ever bring about the redemption of Ireland.'[1] He published his memoirs, *Twenty-five Years in the Secret Service: the Recollections of a Spy*, in 1894. (*Image taken from Henri Le Caron*, Twenty-five Years in the Secret Service: the Recollections of a Spy *(London, 1892)*)

---

1   *The Times Special Commission Report*, XII, pp. 49–50.

Pigott Identifies The Letters

Richard Pigott took his place in the witness stand on 20 February 1889 and, in a remarkably tense encounter, the Parnellite barrister, Charles Russell, exposed Pigott as lying under oath and as the forger of the Parnell letters. In the immediate aftermath of his exposure, Pigott disappeared, as perjury was a criminal offence. He was discovered by police in Madrid, but committed suicide rather than surrender himself.

The Special Commission plodded on for another year, its credibility much weakened and undermined. In the spring of 1890 the final verdict of the commission was that while Parnellism was complicit in a conspiracy to withhold rent during the Land War, *The Times'* allegations of complicity with Irish-American Fenianism were not proven. This was not the definitive vindication the Irish Parliamentary Party had sought, but for opponents of Home Rule the attempt to undermine Irish devolution by tying it to Fenianism was unsuccessful and nothing more than a humiliating and miserable failure, if not a dramatic fiasco. (*Courtesy of the National Library of Ireland*)

CAPTAIN O'SHEA GIVING HIS EVIDENCE

WITNESSES

HARRIET WOOL.

CAROLINE PETHERS.

THE JURY

While Parnell survived the Special Commission, in December 1889 it was revealed that he was having an affair with a married woman, Katherine O'Shea. Filing a petition for divorce, her husband, Captain William O'Shea, named Parnell as an adulterer. The fallout tore the Irish Parliamentary Party asunder and it split into Parnellite and anti-Parnellite factions, greatly weakening the efficacy of the party within parliament and in Ireland.

While the Fenian movement continued to be active in Irish society, it was greatly debilitated and entered a period of forced retirement. (*Courtesy of the National Library of Ireland*)

As the nineteenth century closed and a new era began, the IRB was given a boost with the arrival from America of the veteran Fenian Jeremiah O'Donovan Rossa in 1894 and again in 1905. Receiving the freedom of his native Cork city on his second visit, O'Donovan Rossa lectured about his prison experiences and unveiled a number of Republican monuments. He can be seen in this photograph (*indicated by the arrow*) giving an oration at the Manchester Martyrs memorial in Birr, County Offaly. (*Courtesy of the National Library of Ireland*)

IRISH
NATIONAL AMNESTY ASSOCIATION

ROUND ROOM, ROTUNDA

A GREAT

DEMONSTRATION

WILL BE HELD ON

FRIDAY EVG., OCTOBER 21

To Welcome the Recently

RELEASED POLITICAL PRISONERS

The victims of the infamous Spy and Informer, RED JIM McDERMOTT; after their Fifteen years cruel imprisonment in English Jails,

MESSRS. WILSON, DALTON & FEATHERSTON

Who will leave the Committee Rooms, 41 York St. on that Evening at 7.30, o'clock accompanied by the

CITY BANDS!

And National Bodies, with Torches, and proceed by Stephen's Green, Grafton Street, Westmoreland Street, and O'Connell Street, to the

ROUND ROOM, ROTUNDA

WHEN A GREAT

PUBLIC MEETING

WILL BE HELD AT 8.30 P.M. AT WHICH

MR. MICHAEL LAMBERT

(PRESIDENT OF THE ASSOCIATION)

MISS — Will Preside, supported by — MR.

MAUD GONNE | JAMES F. EGAN

(The Political Prisoners' most Illustrious Advocate). (Ex-Political Prisoner). Amnesty's Great Ambassadors.

MR. J. E. REDMOND, MP.

(The Political Prisoners' National Counsel and Adviser).

SEVERAL IRISH MEMBERS OF PARLIAMENT
MEMBERS OF THE DUBLIN CORPORATION

Of the VARIOUS NATIONAL and TRADE SOCIETIES and OTHER DISTINGUISHED CITIZENS AND FRIENDS OF THE AMNESTY CAUSE THROUGH IRELAND.

ADMISSION FREE!

The Balcony will be Reserved. Tickets for which can be obtained from any of the Members of the Committee, or at the Committee Rooms, 41 York Street

GOD SAVE IRELAND

CORRIGAN & WILSON, Printers, Dublin.

Opposite:

Inspired by the plight of Fenian dynamitards, a strong amnesty campaign was established by the IRB in 1892 to demand their release from British prisons. Led by a number of senior figures within Dublin Fenianism including Fred Allen, Michael Lambert and James Bermingham, the association organised rallies throughout Ireland in support of Fenian prisoners and cared for their dependants. By coincidence the Amnesty Association campaign was given great impetus by an upsurge in national interest on the one-hundredth anniversary of the United Irishmen's rebellion of 1798. The British government released all the imprisoned dynamitards arrested during the Fenian bombing campaign of 1881–85. This poster is a notice of a rally to celebrate the release of Tom Clarke (alias Henry Wilson), Henry Dalton and Timothy Featherstone. (*Courtesy of Aidan Lambert*)

For thirty years Fred Allen was a senior ranking Fenian in Dublin. He had joined the IRB in 1880 and within three years became an organiser in Leinster, actively distributing arms and funds throughout the province. Becoming a member of the Supreme Council, Allen remained active within the IRB until 1912 when he was ousted by a younger generation of conspirators led by the old Fenian Tom Clarke. He enjoyed a lifelong friendship with Major John MacBride, executed for his role in the Easter Rising. Allen was imprisoned during the War of Independence (1919–21) and was held at Mountjoy Prison and Ballykinlar internment camp, County Down. (*Courtesy of Mercier Archive*)

Michael Lambert was a mechanical instrument maker and optician who had been recruited into the IRB before the escape of James Stephens in 1865. He designed the keys for Stephens' escape from Richmond Bridewell and also played a role in the abortive Battle of Tallaght during the Fenian rebellion two years later. In 1896 Lambert was elected president of the Amnesty Association and oversaw the rehabilitation of John Daly, Thomas Clarke and James 'Skin the Goat' Fitzharris, to name a few, upon their release from prison. He worked tirelessly to secure employment for them. A pallbearer at the funeral of James Stephens, he was involved in several nationalist monument committees, fund-raising for projects such as the Parnell monument, the James Stephens monument in Glasnevin Cemetery and the original plan for a Wolfe Tone monument on St Stephen's Green, Dublin. Held in high esteem by the IRB, forty years after the escape of Stephens he was awarded a book and gold watch for his role in that action. Lambert died on 14 August 1908. (*Courtesy of Aidan Lambert*)

THE LATE JAMES BERMINGHAM.

James Bermingham, who fought in the 1867 rebellion and played a role in the Battle of Tallaght in South Dublin, acted as the treasurer of the Amnesty Association and worked for the release of Fenian dynamitards. (*Courtesy of Bernard Bermingham*)

With the outbreak of the second Boer War in 1899, the Fenian conspirators sought to take advantage of British difficulty and organised an Irish regiment to fight with the Boers. Known as the Irish Transvaal Brigade, they were led by a nominal chief, the Irish-American John Blake – 300 men joined the brigade. (*Private collection*)

Major John MacBride was an organiser of the Irish Transvaal Brigade and served as second in command of the unit with the rank of major. The brigade enjoyed great success during the war and their campaigns were widely publicised in Ireland where they were referred to as MacBride's Brigade. MacBride had been active within Fenianism since he was a young man when he joined the Young Ireland Society in Dublin. In 1903 he married Maud Gonne, the daughter of a British Army officer and an ardent Irish Republican. Although not a member of the Irish Volunteers, he joined Thomas MacDonagh on his way to take over Jacob's biscuit factory during the Easter Rising in 1916 and was executed for his involvement. (*Private collection*)

The last of the dynamitards to be released from prison, Thomas Clarke tried to settle in America but returned to Ireland in 1907. In this photograph he can be seen (*on the left*) at a Bodenstown commemoration in 1915 with fellow IRB conspirator Dermot Lynch. His arrival back to Ireland was well judged, as the IRB was undergoing a significant period of reorganisation with younger conspirators seeking to revive the declining organisation. Due to the harsh conditions of his imprisonment, he was revered by the new generation of IRB conspirators as the personification of the Fenian struggle and was co-opted to the Supreme Council as treasurer. Clarke associated with young radicals within the IRB such as Denis McCullough, Bulmer Hobson and most importantly Seán MacDiarmada, and helped them to win control of the IRB from the old guard, which included MacBride and Allen. He set up a tobacco shop at 77 Amiens Street, Dublin and later at 75a Parnell Street. His shop became a hub for revolutionary conspiracy. (*Courtesy of the National Library of Ireland*)

Overleaf:

In 1915 the veteran Fenian Jeremiah O'Donovan Rossa died in St Vincent's Hospital, Staten Island, New York. Learning of his death Clarke sent a telegram to John Devoy requesting that the body be returned to Ireland where it would be buried in Glasnevin Cemetery. Viewing the funeral of the indomitable O'Donovan Rossa as a means of asserting the influence and force of nationalist Ireland, Clarke asked Patrick Pearse to give the graveside oration. Pearse, who had been sworn into the IRB in December 1913, gave an incredibly powerful speech establishing continuity between the Fenians and the newly rejuvenated IRB. He announced, in reference to the British government:

> They think that they have pacified Ireland. They think that they have purchased half of us and intimidated the other half. They think that they have foreseen everything, think that they have provided against everything; but, the fools, the fools, the fools! — They have left us our Fenian dead, and while Ireland holds these graves, Ireland unfree shall never be at peace.

With history coming full circle, it was apparent that Fenianism, through conspirators such as Clarke, had passed the torch of Republican idealism to a new generation, and that generation could not have made the gains it achieved between 1916 and 1921 without the sixty years of extraordinary intrigue, resilience, idealism and self-sacrifice which their predecessors maintained. (*Courtesy of Glasnevin Cemetery*)

SELECT BIBLIOGRAPHY

BOOKS

Anderson, Sir Robert, *Sidelights on the Home Rule Movement* (London, 1906)

Anderson, Sir Robert, *The Lighter Side of My Official Life* (London, 1910)

Anon, *The Repeal of the Union Conspiracy or Mr Parnell M.P. and the IRB* (London, 1886)

Anon, *Parnellism and Crime,* reprinted from *The Times,* revised edition (London, 1887)

Bagenal, Philip, *The American Irish and their Influence on Irish Politics* (London, 1882)

Bahlman, Dudley (ed.), *The Diary of Sir Edward Walter Hamilton* (Oxford, 1972)

Brackenbury, Sir Henry, *Some Memories of My Spare Time 1856–1885* (Edinburgh, 1909)

Bussy, Frederick Moir, *Irish Conspiracies: Recollections of John Mallon* (London, 1910)

Crenshaw, Martha, 'The causes of terrorism', in *Comparative Politics*, 13:4 (July 1981)

Clarke, Thomas J., *Glimpses of an Irish Felon's Prison Life* (Cork, 1970)

Curran, John Adye, *Reminiscences of John Adye Curran* (London, 1914)

D'Arcy, William, *The Fenian Movement in the United States* (Washington, 1947)

Denieffe, Joseph, *A Personal Narrative of the Irish Revolutionary Brotherhood* (New York, 1906)

Devoy, John, 'The Story of the Clan na Gael', *Gaelic American* (29 November 1924)

Devoy, John, *Recollections of an Irish Rebel* (New York, 1929)

Hall, J. B., *Random Records of a Reporter* (Dublin, 1928)

Henry, George, 'An American view of Ireland', in *Nineteenth Century: A Monthly Review*, 12:66 (August 1882)

Kee, Robert, *The Green Flag: a History of Irish Nationalism* (London, 1972)

Kenna, Shane, *War in the Shadows: The Irish-American Fenians Who Bombed Victorian Britain* (Dublin, 2014)

Le Caron, Henri, *Twenty-five Years in the Secret Service: the Recollections of a Spy* (London, 1892)

Le Roux, Louis, *Tom Clarke and the Irish Freedom Movement* (Dublin, 1936)

McConville, Seán, *Irish Political Prisoners, 1848–1922: Theatres of War* (London, 2005)

Moody, T. W. and O'Broin, Leon, 'The IRB Supreme Council, 1868–78: Selected Documents' in T. W. Moody (ed.) *Irish Historical Studies*, Vol. XIX (1974–75)

O'Brien, William and Ryan, Desmond (eds), *Devoy's Post Bag*, Vol. 1 (Dublin, 1948)

O Broin, Leon, *The Prime Informer: A Suppressed Scandal* (London, 1971)

Ó Luing, Seán, *The Catalpa Rescue* (Tralee, 1965)

Pearse, Patrick, 'A character study', in *Diarmuid Ó Donnabain Rosa 1831–1915: Souvenir of Public Funeral to Glasnevin Cemetery, Dublin, 1 August 1915* (Dublin, 1915)

Report on Special Commission 1888 [C-5891], H.C. 1890

Ryan, Desmond, *The Phoenix Flame: A Study of Fenianism and John Devoy* (London, 1937)

Ryan, Desmond, *The Fenian Chief: A Biography of James Stephens* (Dublin, 1967)

Ryan, Mark F., *Fenian Memories* (Dublin, 1945)

Short, K. R. M., *The Dynamite War: Irish-American Bombers in Victorian Britain* (Dublin, 1979)

Sullivan T. D., *Recollections of Troubled Times in Irish Politics* (Dublin, 1905)

The Annual Register: a review of public events at home and abroad for the year 1881 (London, 1882)

Tynan, Patrick, *The Irish National Invincibles and Their Times* (London, 1894)

NEWSPAPERS

The Aberdeen Weekly Journal

The Belfast Newsletter

The Birmingham Daily Post

The Chronicle

The Daily News

The Freeman's Journal

The Glasgow Herald

The Graphic

The Hull Packet and East Riding Times

The Illustrated Police News

Irish Freedom

The Irishman

The Irish Times

Irish Weekly Independent

The Irish World

The Labour World

The Leeds Mercury

The Liverpool Mercury

Lloyds Weekly Newspaper

The London Illustrated News

The Manchester Times

The Nation

The New York Times

The Newcastle Courant

The North British Daily Mail

The Northern Echo

The Pall Mall Gazette

The Penny Illustrated

The Preston Guardian

Reynolds Weekly newspaper

The Sligo Champion

The Times

The Weekly Freeman

The Western Mail

INDEX

61st (South Gloucestershire) Regiment 43
69th Division 18, 19
1798 United Irishmen rebellion 11, 147
1848 rebellion 7, 8, 14
1867 rebellion 53, 55–57, 59, 65, 70, 126, 148

A

Abberline, Inspector 129
Allen, Fred 147, 150
Allen, William 62–64
Amnesty Association 71, 147, 148
Anderson, Robert 137
Anthony, George Smith 83
Archdeacon, George 32
Ashe, Thomas 12

B

Bailey, Bernard 99
Ballam, Elizabeth 129
Ballykinlar internment camp 147
Barrett, Michael 68
Barton, Robert 90, 91
Battle of Ridgeway 41
Bermingham, James 147, 148
Blake, John 149
Boer War 11, 126, 149
Brackenbury, Henry 104, 105, 137
Brady, Joe 100, 110
Breslin, John 36, 81, 83
Brett, Colonel 45
Brett, James 62
Brooklyn dynamite school 89, 120
Broughton, Henry 29
Burke, Morgan 34
Burke, Sub-Inspector 53
Burke, Thomas Henry 101–103, 106, 110, 112–114, 136, 138
Butt, Isaac 71, 77
Byrne, Daniel 36
Byrne, Frank 95, 98, 99

C

Caffery, Thomas 113
Callan, Thomas 135
Canada 39–42, 118
Carey, James 96, 98, 99, 109, 110, 115, 116, 118
Carey, Peter 109
Carroll, William 84
Casey, Joseph 66, 67
Catalpa 11, 80, 83
Cavanagh, Samuel 71
Cavendish, Lord Frederick 101, 102, 106, 110, 112, 113, 136, 138
Ceannt, Éamonn 12
Charing Cross 121, 122
Chester Castle 49–51, 98
Clan na Gael 10, 11, 71, 72, 80, 84, 87, 88, 119, 127, 130, 131
Clarke, Thomas James 12, 119, 126, 147, 148, 150, 151
Clerkenwell 66–68
Cluseret, Gustave Paul 48, 56
Cohen, Joseph 135
Collins, Jerome 71, 72
Collins, Michael 12
Constitution of the IRB 73
Corcoran, Michael 18
Corydon, John Joseph 49
Costello, Augustine 60, 61
Courtney, Bryan 60, 61
Cranston, Robert 78, 79, 83
Cuba Five 71, 76
Cullen, Cardinal Paul 10
Cunningham, James Gilbert 129
Curley, Daniel 100, 110, 111
Curran, John Adye 106

D

Dalton, Henry 120, 147
Daly, Edward 126

Daly, John 126, 148
Darragh, Thomas 78, 79, 83
Davis, Thomas 72
Davitt, Michael 51
Deasy, Timothy 62
Denieffe, Joseph 8, 9
Desmond, Timothy 68
Desmond, Tom 81, 83
Desmond, William 68
Devoy, John 11, 43, 44, 49, 71, 76, 78, 81, 84, 85, 151
Dillon, Brian 27
Doheny, Michael 8, 15
Dowling Mulcahy, Denis 23, 31
Dublin Castle 65, 101, 104, 115
Dublin Metropolitan Police 106
Duggan, Thomas 27
Dunne, James 58
Dynamite Saturday 128

E

Easter Rising 11, 12, 126, 147, 149
Emmet Monument Association (EMA) 8, 9, 17
Emmet, Robert 62, 72
English, Nicholas 68
Erin's Hope 59, 60

F

Fagan, Michael 100, 112
Fariola, Octave 56
Farrell, Robert 107
Featherstone, Timothy 147
Fenian Brotherhood 10, 17–19, 23, 39, 59, 72
Fenian dynamitards 90, 119–21, 125–129, 134–136, 147, 148, 150
Finn, Edward 30
Fitzharris, James 108, 109, 148
Fleming, John 127
Flood, John 50
Foley, Patrick 44
Forster, William 92, 101
Fort Erie 41

Freemantle 11, 50, 57, 78, 80, 81, 83

G

Gallagher, Thomas 119, 120
Gavan Duffy, Charles 8
George, Herbert 129
Gladstone, William Ewart 71, 89, 132, 133
Glasnevin Cemetery 12, 103, 148, 151
Gonne, Maud 108, 149

H

Hanley, John 60, 61
Hanlon, Joseph 114
Hanlon, Lawrence 114
Harkins, Michael 135
Harrington, Michael 78, 83
Hassett, Thomas 78, 83
Haybourne, Patrick 31
Hobson, Bulmer 11, 12, 150
Hogan, Martin 78, 79, 83
Home Rule 132–134, 136, 137, 143
House of Commons 128, 138
Hughes, John 32

I

Irish National Invincibles 11, 96–100, 102, 106–109, 111, 113, 114, 117
Irish National Land League 87, 93, 141
Irish Parliamentary Party 11, 84, 130–132, 134–137, 141–144
Irish Republican Army 122
Irish Republican Brotherhood (IRB) 7, 9, 10, 11, 15–17, 23, 25, 31, 32, 36, 43, 49–51, 53, 65–67, 70–73, 87, 95, 98, 108, 118, 145, 147, 148, 150, 151
Irish Tenants League 8
Irish Transvaal Brigade 149

J

Jenkinson, Edward George 105, 118, 137
Jubilee plot 134–136

K

Kavanagh, John F. 60